THE MANY LOVES OF BUFFALO BILL

The True Story of Life on the Wild West Show

Chris Enss
Foreword by Peter Sherayko

TWODOT

GUILFORD, CONNECTICUT
HELENA, MONTANA

AN IMPRINT OF GLOBE PEQUOT PRESS

A · T W O D O T® · B O O K

TwoDot is an imprint of Globe Pequot Press and a registered trademark of Morris Book Publishing, LLC.

Project editor: Jessica Haberman
Text design: Sheryl P. Kober

Library of Congress Cataloging-in-Publication Data

Enss, Chris, 1961–
  The many loves of Buffalo Bill : the true story of life on the Wild West
    show / Chris Enss ; foreword by Peter Sherayko.
      p. cm.
  Includes bibliographical references and index.
  ISBN 978-0-7627-4815-0
  1. Buffalo Bill, 1846–1917. 2. Buffalo Bill, 1846–1917—Relations with
    women. 3. Pioneers—West (U.S.)—Biography. 4. Entertainers—
    United States—Biography. I. Title.
  F594.B94.E57 2010
  978'.02092—dc22
  [B]

                                                    2009034233

Printed in the United States of America

10 9 8 7 6 5 4 3 2 1

CONTENTS

———•———

Acknowledgments . . . . *iv*

Foreword by Peter Sherayko . . . . *v*

Introduction . . . . *ix*

ONE: Man of the Family *1*

TWO: The Courtship of Louisa *13*

THREE: Husband, Father, Scout, and Actor *25*

FOUR: Life in the Limelight *40*

FIVE: The Dear Favorite *55*

SIX: Away from Home *61*

SEVEN: The Lady of Venice *75*

EIGHT: The Cody Trials *85*

NINE: A Wandering Heart *99*

TEN: The Sharpshooter *108*

ELEVEN: The Final Ride *116*

Notes *129*

Bibliography *141*

Index *144*

About the Author *150*

ACKNOWLEDGMENTS

It takes the help of many to write a book of this nature. It is with that in mind that I express my deep sense of appreciation to individuals and organizations for their kind and generous assistance in the preparation of this work. Without such help and cooperation, the gathering of much valuable data would have been all but impossible.

The kindness of librarians, historical society directors, representatives of the National Archives and Record Service, various newspaper staff members, and others in allowing me to review and duplicate important documents has aided significantly in the compiling of interesting biographical material. To these organizations and individuals, I wish to extend my heartfelt thanks: the staff at the Buffalo Bill Historical Center and the McCracken Research Library—in particular Mary Robinson; Judy Logan at the Garst Museum in Greenville, Ohio; the morgue departments at the *Chicago Tribune* and the *New York Times*; the South Dakota State Historical Society in Pierre, South Dakota; the Missouri History Museum; and Mary Ann Trygg and the staff at the Nevada County Madelyn Helling Library.

And to these individuals, many of whom have given most generously of their time, thank you so much: actor Peter Sherayko, historian Ron Sturgell, Howard Kazanjian, Stephanie Rogers, my editor Erin Turner, the art department at Globe Pequot Press, and Barrett Williams.

FOREWORD

———•———

I've got a good woman—what's the matter with me?
What makes me want to love every woman I see?
—HANK WILLIAMS JR.

In 1883 a remote cow town in Nebraska was treated to the grand opening of a show that would reign as America's favorite for thirty years. It was Buffalo Bill's Wild West. Bill Cody played Buffalo Bill professionally for more than forty years, a role that probably will never be topped.

In 1900 the *Who, What and Where* book published hundreds of photos and biographies of kings, presidents, world leaders in business, and other famous people. Buffalo Bill is the only personality from America's western frontier. Daniel Boone, Davy Crockett, Jesse James, General George Custer, Billy the Kid, Wild Bill Hickok—not one of them appeared in these pages. Only William F. Cody—Buffalo Bill—received that honor. His fame was so wide that he ranked with the most powerful men of all time. Virtually every American knew of Buffalo Bill: how he earned his nickname, rode for the Pony Express, fought and befriended Indians, scouted for the U.S. Army in both the Civil War and Indian wars, and performed for ten seasons as a professional actor—all before the age of forty.

When he created his Wild West Exhibition, Cody gave his audience their money's worth: wild Indians, fancy roping, and deadeye marksmanship. But Bill himself topped them all, shooting his rifle from horseback at a full gallop and breaking dozens of glass balls thrown into the air. The crowd loved it, and so did the press and dime novelists, with writers such as

Mark Twain praising the show. In short, he out-Barnumed P. T. Barnum. The exhibition set attendance records throughout the United States and Europe.

More than a hundred books and articles have been written about Cody the frontiersman and entertainer. What more could be said? Well, in *The Many Loves of Buffalo Bill,* Chris Enss has uncovered another notch in the Shakespearean life of Bill Cody. Yes, Cody was a showman, a frontiersman, a man whose life started during the Mexican-American War and ended just as the United States entered "the war to end all wars," World War I. Yet he was a man, a man in the truest sense of the word, one who cut his own trail and followed his own spirit guide. As a boy, he marveled at men like Kit Carson, who taught him how to shoot from horseback, and Jim Bridger, who taught him Indian sign language. As a ten-year-old he dreamed of becoming one of his buckskin-clad heroes, and by golly by gum, he did. But he was tainted with the sins of man: an eye for beauty and strength; an admirer of courage and adventure; and in some circles, a weakness for cigars, whiskey, and women. In his own words, "Yeah, I like my cigars and whiskey and I sure do love those women."

Chris Enss gives us the stories behind many of the beauties who captivated Buffalo Bill. She gives us a clearer insight into a simple yet complicated man—the showman Buffalo Bill and the man Bill Cody. Yet for all of his fame, money, and problems, he was a complex hero, and Chris Enss gives us some clues and answers to his character. It's great how writers and researchers uncover questions that so many of us curious followers of American history have. My hat is always doffed and a glass is raised to the hero of the West, Buffalo Bill, and now, thanks to Chris—a glass is raised to her.

Chris Enss is truly a woman of the West. Her previous books, mostly about women of the frontier West, are enjoyable and informative. We met several years ago at a mutual book signing in Tombstone, Arizona. I was impressed not only by her charm and style but also by her incredible knowledge and passion for what Buffalo Bill called "God's biggest playground." We are indeed lucky today that a whole new breed of people are influencing, educating, and entertaining those of us who are interested in American history. Chris Enss is truly one who has blessed us with her knowledge and passion for stories of the West that haven't been, but need to be, told.

RIDE HARD AND SHOOT STRAIGHT!
—PETER SHERAYKO

Buffalo Bill at twenty-three years old (1869)
Buffalo Bill Historical Center, Cody, WY, P.69.189

INTRODUCTION

———•———

If he isn't a pet with the women he ought to be.
—OBSERVATION FROM A FEMALE NEWSPAPER REPORTER,
J. M. W., IN AN ARTICLE ENTITLED "COLONEL CODY TALKS" (1894)

A sea of elegantly dressed, excited guests lined the hallway of a refined hotel in Omaha, Nebraska. The buzz of conversation was deafening as they clustered into an open door leading to a gigantic suite. Waiters in tails and white gloves and carrying trays of champagne-filled glasses weaved around the congregation. It was the winter of 1877, and people from all walks of life were at the posh inn. Entertainers, businessmen and -women, cattle barons, and politicians helped themselves to the abundance of wine and toasted one another's good fortune.

The chatter and drinks were set aside when the guest of honor arrived on the scene. The entire room was galvanized into a tumultuous applause as thirty-one-year-old William F. Cody entered and made his way through the crowd. He smiled appreciatively in response to the enthusiastic welcome. Standing six feet one inch tall, the man was draped in a tuxedo-style waistcoat, vest, and perfectly pressed trousers.[1] His dark, curly, shoulder-length hair, thin mustache, and small goatee completed his handsome, polished look.

Beautiful women in taffeta gowns and lace bonnets jockeyed for a place beside him. He reveled in the attention and politely allowed one of the coquettish disciples to slide her dainty arm into the crook of his.

He held the audience that had gathered around him captive with his genteel manner and fascinating tales of life on the wild frontier. "I was fourteen when I signed on as one of the Pony Express riders," William proudly announced. "They argued that I was too young for the job, but I insisted I could do it, and finally they gave me the shortest route, a ride of thirty-five miles with three changes of ponies."[2] William explained to the crowd that he rode seventy miles every day for three months. "When it became apparent to the men in charge that the boys could do better than forty-five miles a day the stretches were lengthened," he continued. "The pay of the rider was from $100 to $125 a month. It was announced that the further a man rode the better would be his pay. . . . In stretching my own route I found myself getting further and further west. I never was quite sure when I started out when I should reach my destination or whether I should never reach it at all."

William's admirers gushed and commended him for his service. As he was graciously accepting the praise, his wife, Louisa, entered the room from an adjoining suite and faded inconspicuously into the crowd. She surveyed the inspired faces watching her husband, taking particular notice of the ladies flanking him on either side. The petite, porcelain-skinned woman fought to maintain her composure as one of the brazen ladies leaned in closely to William and whispered in his ear. He grinned a schoolboy grin and casually glanced around the room. His expression changed slightly when his eyes met Louisa's.[3]

The occasion for this well-attended event was a farewell party for William's theatrical troupe. The couple's marriage, already strained because of months of separation, was further harassed by rumors of infidelity. Louisa had spent the better part of her relationship with William struggling with insecurities.[4] Vying for his attention were the vast, untamed plains, the love of adventure and scouting, and the intoxicating limelight. At the beginning of their marriage, she had tried to get him to settle into a predictable and steady life-

William F. Cody surrounded by cowgirls from the 101 Ranch
Buffalo Bill Historical Center, Cody, WY, P.69.854

style. William made a valiant effort. He purchased an inn in Leavenworth, Kansas, and tended to the needs of travelers passing through. His overly generous nature nearly brought the business to ruin, however. Guests with little or no money were allowed to stay at the hotel for free, and meals were included in the price.[5]

In addition to William's abysmal business practices, there was another hint of his restlessness: an absent, far-off expression that lingered in his eyes. Louisa's sympathy for his passion to travel was heightened by the many books on the subject of frontier life. Knowing he would never be truly happy as a landlord, she released him from the obligation of the inn and sent him back to work on the open range. In the decade since that time, William had been appointed Chief of Scouts for the Fifth U.S. Cavalry, won the Medal of Honor with George Custer, and hunted buffalo for the railroad, subsequently earning him the nickname Buffalo Bill. Along with those accomplishments, William and the dime novelist Ned Buntline formed a successful theatrical troupe with Bill Hickok and Texas Jack Omohundro called the Buffalo Bill Combination.

Reports in newspapers and magazines about William's many heroic deeds helped make him famous from coast to coast. Such notoriety brought more demands on his time. Home and family were sandwiched between jobs such as scouting for the military and performances onstage and in lecture halls.

Louisa resigned herself to waiting supportively in the background while William shared his exciting exploits with an adoring public, but she resented the overt attention of many of the women in his sphere of influence. Against warring Indians, inhospitable terrains, and wild animals, he was a strong, resilient man, but he was vulnerable to charming female supporters.

The party was in full swing, and Louisa helped herself to a glass of wine and occasionally chatted with a guest or two. The evening progressed without a clear opportunity for her to be in William's immediate orbit. The festivities slowly wound down, and one by one the guests said their good-byes and left the hotel suite. Undaunted by the late hour, William continued to hold court with the actresses who had been with him throughout the night. Eventually, they too realized it was time to go and bade farewell to their host by kissing him on the cheek. Louisa's eyes were glued to the scene. She was shocked by such a public display and even more so when she saw William return the women's kisses.[6]

Louisa pushed through the dwindling group of partygoers and marched over to William. He could see she was upset and attempted to calm her distressed demeanor. She disregarded his attempt to talk to her and loudly scolded him for his insensitive behavior. A hush fell over the room, and only Louisa's heated words rose above the quiet. William handled the intense, embarrassing exchange with as much dignity as he could muster. After she spoke her mind, Louisa stormed out of the room. William watched his wife walk away; then he turned his attention to the uncomfortable guests and wished them well as they made their way out.

Looking back on the incident years later, William didn't understand why Louisa objected to the simple gestures of appreciation. "I do not think most wives would have felt a little angry to know and hear her husband in an adjoining room on Sunday morning, drinking beer and kissing theatrical girls of his company," he wrote in his memoirs. "I think they would have been rather proud of a husband who had six or seven months work with a party of people who were in his employ, to know and feel that they were on a kindly footing. . . . Not one of them got up and kissed papa goodbye, but all four of them rushed up and kissed papa, their old manager, goodbye."[7]

The Codys made the trip from Omaha to their home in North Platte, Nebraska, with barely a word spoken between them. Both were occupied with their own thoughts. William was only nineteen when they had met, but he had already lived more life than most men twice his age. Louisa liked that about him, and although she would never readily admit it, she knew that was a big part of what drew other women to him as well.

William Frederick Cody was born on February 26, 1846, in Scott County, Iowa, near the little town of LeClaire. His parents, Isaac and Mary Ann, had seven children total, four girls and three boys. Isaac was an adventurer at heart and, in 1850, set out for California to take part in the Gold Rush. After hearing stories from prospectors returning from California about how difficult it was to find gold, Isaac decided against going west. He decided instead to relocate his family to a homestead near Fort Leavenworth, Kansas.

The first visit to the fort stirred a desire in Bill to travel and explore unsettled lands. "The Cavalry—or dragoons as they called them then," William wrote in his autobiography, "were engaged in saber drills, their swords flashing in the sunlight. Artillery was rumbling over the parade ground. Infantry was marching and wheeling. About the Post were men dressed all in buckskin with coonskin caps or broad-brimmed slough hats—real Westerners of whom I had dreamed. Indians of all sorts were loafing about—all friendly, but a new and different kind of Indian from any I had seen. Kickapoos, Possawatomies, Delawares, Choctaws, and other tribes of which I had often heard. Everything I saw fascinated me."[8]

The pull to leave home and head west was great, but Mary Ann convinced the seven-year-old boy to content himself with life on a farm until he was a bit older. Life in the Salt Creek Valley wasn't without excitement. Bill grew up in the midst of Indians and the wild life of the plains as well as in the very thick of the early fights that occurred between northerners and southerners over the question of slavery.

Isaac Cody took a firm stand against slavery and was persecuted for his position. Southern sympathizers threatened his life and that of his family if they didn't leave Kansas. Isaac refused to go, and as a result his wife and children were forced to hide from groups sent to kill them. Bill, who was an expert with a gun by that time, thwarted an attempt by pro-slavery leaders to steal his prize pony and shoot his father. Isaac was stabbed shortly after the incident, however, and eventually died from the wound.

"I was only eleven years old," William later wrote, "and the only man of the family. I made up my mind to be a bread winner."[9]

Young William found work with the freighting company Russell, Majors and Waddell. He helped herd the extra cattle that followed the wagon trains en route to deliver supplies to soldiers in the field. The route originated in St. Joseph, Missouri, and ended in San Francisco. William was exposed to a life of danger as the train was often assaulted by Indians and outlaws. He frequently had to help defend the cargo, shooting it out with Cheyenne, Arapaho, and Sioux warriors or with highway robbers.

During his first trip with the company, he stopped an ambush by Indians encamped west of Fort Kearney near Plum Creek. William spotted the outline of an Indian and his headdress against the backdrop of a full moon. "I knew well enough that in another second he would drop one of my friends," he remembered in his memoirs. "So I raised my Yaeger and fired. I saw the figure collapse, and heard it come tumbling thirty feet down the bank, landing with a splash in the water." By the time the train returned to Fort Leavenworth, news of William's exploits had reached his family, friends, and neighbors. A reporter with the *Leavenworth Times* interviewed the boy and published a story about him that proclaimed William Cody to be the "youngest Indian slayer on the plains."

Having proven to himself and his elders that his future lay in being a frontiersman, he returned to the plains. Among the varied events he experienced were losing a caravan of goods to the Mormon leader Lot Smith and his followers, meeting and spending time with celebrated scouts and Indian hunters Kit Carson and Jim Bridger, as well as trapping beaver and mink along the waterways in the Rockies. While tending to his traps on Prairie Creek, he came face to face with a bear that had killed one of his oxen and a bull. William shot the bear, saving himself, his partner, and their livestock from further attack.

On one occasion William broke his leg during a hunting expedition in the wilderness and was forced to hole up in a cave for more than twenty days waiting for help to arrive. After a stint riding for the Pony Express, he took a job supplying meat for the Kansas Pacific Railroad as a buffalo hunter.

In an eighteen-month period he killed 4,280 buffalo. He then joined a campaign with Wild Bill Hickok to track down warring bands of Indians and subdue them. At the conclusion of that venture, he offered his expertise to the government and became a guide for the Ninth Kansas Cavalry.

In 1864 William enlisted in the army. He was eighteen years old.[10]

During William's long absences working for the military under General Phil Sheridan in the Indian wars and eventually reenacting his life onstage across the country, Louisa maintained their home and cared for their children. Occasionally she would attend one of Buffalo Bill's shows. William appreciated Louisa's presence at his performances. He made a point of locating her in the audience and calling out her name. "He came forward, leaned over the gas footlights and waved his arms," she recalled.

"Oh, Mamma!" he shouted. "I'm a bad actor!" The house roared. Will threw her a kiss and then leaned forward again while the house stilled. "Honest, Mamma," he shouted, "does this look as awful out there as it feels up here?" Once more the house chuckled and applauded. Someone called out the fact that Louisa was Mrs. Buffalo Bill.

Once the crowd realized that it was indeed William's wife he was addressing, the audience cheered and tried to coax Louisa on stage. Embarrassed and nervous, she refused. It wasn't until William held his hand out to her that she relented. "Come on up. You can't be any worse scared than I am," Louisa recalled William saying.[11]

"Someone placed a chair in the orchestra pit," she added. "Hands reached to help, and I was boosted onto the stage, and Arta after me. I was plainly frightened and it showed. 'Now you can understand how hard your poor old husband [he was twenty-six years old] has to work to make a living!'" William boomed. The audience again applauded, and William joined them. "After that," Louisa reported, "whenever I went to see my husband's show, I chose a seat in the farthest and darkest part of the house. But it did little good. For invariably Will would seek me out, and call 'Hello, Mamma. Oh, but I'm a bad actor.'"[12]

Both Louisa and William remembered those moments with great fondness. As his theatrical career advanced, William concentrated less and less on wife and home. He was preoccupied with creating a bigger program that celebrated the history of the frontier and with becoming an international showman.

Louisa was loyal to William and, according to a close friend, "loved him more than most women loved their husbands." She demonstrated her deep affection for him by spending hours making the elaborate costumes he liked to wear. She was an exceptional seamstress and made the patterns, selected materials, and stitched together the fringed jackets and gauntlets that became William's trademark. She tried to make him understand how much she wanted him to spend more time with her. She felt that if he truly grasped her longing, he would be more inclined to turn down the advancements made by other women.

The tension between William and Louisa continued long after the stormy, uncomfortable scene at the farewell party in Omaha had passed. For the bulk of their marriage, Louisa fretted over the women who flung themselves at William, the expense of his various love affairs, the potential scandal, and the alienation of affection that followed.

Not only did the many loves of Buffalo Bill Cody threaten to break up his marriage, but several of William's friends predicted that Louisa's intolerance of his roving eye would ultimately "bust up the Wild West."

ONE

Man of the Family

As the head of the household he wanted to be called Bill. A compromise was worked out: to most of his friends he was Bill, to his family—especially his mother—he was Billy.

—JULIA CODY GOODMAN (1922)

Twelve-year-old William Cody plunged a meaty fist into the eye of nineteen-year-old Steven Gobel and watched him fall backward onto the ground. Every student in the Salt Creek Valley School in LeClaire, Iowa, had vacated the one-room building to watch the two boys fight. Most were cheering for William, but some were cheering for Steven. Among them was a pretty, doe-eyed girl named Mary Hyatt. William scanned the sea of faces around him, searching for Mary. When he found her, the two shared a smile. It was obvious the pair were smitten with each other. The exchange did not go unnoticed by Steven, who also was fond of Mary. He leaped to his feet and lunged at William.

The young men tumbled over, and Steven punched William repeatedly in the ribs. The scrappy Steven clearly had the advantage because of his size and age, but William was determined not to be bested.

To win Mary's favor and strike a blow against the class bully, who made a sport of tormenting many of the younger pupils, William had to stand his ground. Somewhere in the midst of the frustrating struggle, William pulled out a Bowie knife and stuck it into the lower part of his opponent's leg. Blood gushed from the wound, and Steven screamed in terror. "I've been killed," he cried out to the horrified students looking on.[1] William was confident that the gash would not cause any permanent damage.

William had learned about hunting and skinning all types of animals while riding with the Russell, Majors and Waddell freight company. He knew the difference between a life-threatening cut and one that merely required stitches. William was unable to reassure his awestruck fellow students that Steven would be fine. Steven continued to yell, and his friends pressed in around him with rags trying to stop the bleeding. The majority of students felt that William's actions were extreme, and sentiments quickly turned against him. Even Mary, whose affections he most coveted, now focused all her attention on the wounded Steven.

A few of the students hurried off to get the teacher, and William quickly contemplated his next move. The teacher was a hard man who strongly believed in corporal punishment.

William was frequently beaten with a hazel switch for what the instructor felt was general lack of respect. The routine paddling brought tears to Mary's eyes. William endured the harsh treatment because his mother desperately wanted him to get an education, and there were no other schools in the area from which to choose. He fully anticipated being expelled for his actions, but not before the teacher had used another switch on him. In spite of the desire to please his mother, William believed that under the circumstances he'd be better off away from the institution.

As he fled the scene, he met up with the wagon master for Russell, Majors and Waddell. He told the teamster what had happened, and the man was outraged to hear of the behavior of Steven Gobel and the unsympathetic teacher. He offered to return to the school with William in tow and fight the pair himself. William reluctantly agreed. The wagon master pounded on the schoolhouse door with the butt of his revolver and then invited the teacher and the bully to step outside. The teacher refused, dismissed the class, and raced home.

Mary's eyes were trained on William as she left the building. He watched her walk away with a sweet longing, happily anticipating the next time he would see her.[2]

Between Cody's earliest infatuation and the woman who ultimately became his wife were five particular females who doted on him day and night. Martha, Julia, Eliza, Laura Ella (also known as Helen), and Mary (also known as May) were his sisters, and they regarded Cody as a "tender, caring character with true nobility."[3] The tragic 1853 death of Cody's twelve-year-old brother, Samuel, inspired an overly protective attitude in his mother and sisters toward William.[4] According to his sister Helen's biography,

> *The older girls petted Will; the younger regarded him as a superior being; while to all it seemed so fit and proper that the promise of the stars concerning his future should be fulfilled that never for a moment did we weaken in our belief that great things were in store for our only brother.*[5]

Cody possessed a natural talent with firearms and horseback riding. His father, Isaac, recognized his son's ability and nurtured his skills, teaching him how to track and hunt. At the age of seven, William helped escort his family's prairie schooner from Kansas to Platte County, Missouri. Armed with a Sharps rifle, he was ready to defend his loved ones from wild animals and hostile Indians.[6]

In the evenings he helped make camp and provide game for the meals. He thrived on responsibility and had an instinct for obtaining water, striking trails, and finding desirable camping grounds. Cody's sisters and little brother, Charles Whitney (born in 1855), admired his skills and looked to him

Barely three years old, William F. Cody poses for the camera sporting curls and an embroidered jacket, circa 1849
Buffalo Bill Historical Center, Cody, WY, P.6.672

as a protector when their father was away on business. When Isaac passed away in April 1857, William assumed the role as head of the family and proved to his sisters that their trust in him had not been misplaced.[7]

On more than one occasion, William came to his sisters' rescue. In 1854 six-year-old Eliza and four-year-old Helen ventured away from the homestead with the family dog to collect wildflowers for their ailing mother. When they didn't return in a timely fashion, William was sent to find them. When he finally located them, they were being stalked by a panther.

The Codys' dog had dug a place for the youngsters to hide and had fought back the cat, but the panther eventually overpowered the dog. Just as the panther was set to pounce on the girls, William shot the animal and killed it. Eliza and Helen rushed to their brother and threw their arms around his neck in gratitude.[8] "Will, himself but a child, caressed and soothed us in a most paternal fashion," Helen later wrote in her memoirs. "Our brother was our reliance in every emergency."[9]

Cody's mother, Mary Ann, adored William and depended heavily on his resourcefulness. Having lost her firstborn son and her husband, she was vulnerable and despondent. Her emotional despair was compounded by the financial crisis that occurred shortly after her husband's funeral. Ruthless creditors claimed that Isaac owed them thousands of dollars for building supplies used to maintain the ranch. It was through the efforts of her steady and capable son that Mary Ann was able to afford to fight the bogus claims and keep her children fed and clothed.[10] The $45 a month in wages William earned as an extra working for the Russell, Majors and Waddell freight service was used to support his mother, sisters, and brother. "The cares and responsibilities laid upon our brother's shoulders did not quench his boyish spirits and love of fun," Helen remembered. "When he was home he teased us all and roughhoused with Charles and the neighbor's children."[11]

William spent much of his time between jobs tending to herds of cattle on a wagon train, working for the Pony Express, and reenacting Wild West adventures with his siblings. Armed with wooden tomahawks, spears, and guns, William would perform Indian battles and stage robberies. He portrayed the brave protector fighting off bad guys and scalping violent Indians. He enjoyed the masquerade so much that he told his family that when he was older, he planned to run a show portraying life on the rugged frontier.

The men William met during his employment—such as Alec Majors, owner of the Russell, Majors and Waddell freight service, and Kit Carson—acted as surrogate fathers to him and served as examples of how to be a parent to his brother and sisters.[12] Not only did he entertain his younger siblings, but he sometimes acted as disciplinarian as well. "To tell the truth," Helen recorded in her memoirs, "when we misbehaved and Will would crook his finger at us, we would bawl. Yet we fairly worshipped him," she added, "and cried harder when he went away than when he was home."[13]

William's mother and sisters were not the only females of note in his early years. Frank and Bill McCarthy, two of the men he worked for at Russell, Majors and Waddell, had a sister named Sarah with whom he was infatuated. She was older, and he was captivated by her beauty and kindness. "I was 'dead in love' in a juvenile way," William recounted in his autobiography. His feelings for Sarah were never returned, but he came in contact with other girls who took an interest in him. Despite his sister's claim that William was a ladies' man, none of the girls he met captured his attention as much as the untamed frontier.

All of his sisters encouraged his natural love for western adventure, but none more so than Helen Cody Wetmore.

Not only did she listen enthusiastically to William's dreams of traveling beyond the Mississippi to hunt and

With Russel, Majors and Waddell · Col. Cody as a Bullwhacker · Age 11

At 14 · a Pony Express Rider

Two rarely published photographs of William F. Cody from his youth. Top photo is Cody at age eleven from his days as a bullwhacker. Bottom photo is Buffalo Bill at the age of fourteen when he rode for the Pony Express. BuffaPo Bill Historical Center, Cody, WY, P.69.11

trap wild game while riding with Indian warriors, but when they got older, she also helped him shape the real tales he'd experienced into best-selling books. When Helen grew up, she became a writer, ran a newspaper, and guided William's career as a published author working for the creator of the well-known dime novel series, Ned Buntline. The success of the novels gave William the audience he needed to launch his Wild West show.

After William's father died, he often spoke of joining the military. Although Helen would have hated to see him leave home, she supported his desire to serve his country. William's mother, however, made him promise that he would not enlist until she passed away because she couldn't stand the thought of losing another loved one. True to his promise, he waited to sign up with the Seventh Kansas until after his mother's death.[14]

Mary Ann passed away in 1863. The youngest Cody son died less than a year later, at the age of nine.[15] William's sister Julia, who was two years older than he, assumed the role of caring for the younger children. Martha, the oldest daughter, who was nine years William's senior, had preceded their mother in death shortly after she married in 1858.

William admired Julia's willingness to be the matriarch of the family, and he trusted her in ways he never did his other siblings. In her later years she managed his ranch in North Platte, Nebraska, and the Irma Hotel in Cody, Wyoming.

Julia married Al Goodman in late 1862 and was in the process of establishing her own home when the Codys' mother passed away. She put her own plans on hold and focused on raising her siblings. Throughout the course of his life, William wrote Julia letters praising her dedication and devotion. In a letter dated February 14, 1886, he wrote, "Dear Good Sister, your kind letter just received and it proves how good you are—still looking to my interest, and willing to sacrifice your own comfort for my benefit."[16]

On June 14, 1905, more than forty years after his mother died, he continued to sing his sister's praises in his correspondence. "Dear Sister Julia, you have always been good to me. I only wish that someday I will be able to do much more for you. And all my sisters who have been good and true to me."[17]

Julia was one of William's closest friends and confidants, but he was dutiful to his three other sisters. His sister Eliza Alice, the middle Cody daughter, married George Meyers when she was very young. The couple made their home in Jackson County, Kansas. The Meyerses' income was modest, and they could not afford any frills.[18] Once William began to see a profit from the Wild West show, he helped provide the family with funds to travel and visit him in North Platte. Eliza died in 1902 and was buried in Denison, Kansas.[19]

Mary Hannah, more commonly known as May, was the youngest and most daring of the Cody sisters. Until she was grown and married, she and Helen lived with William and Louisa.[20] May was with her brother and sister-in-law at Fort McPherson, Nebraska, when William accepted an appointment by the government as judge of the area. She watched him perform a wedding as one of his first acts of duty. At the conclusion of the ceremony, May proudly congratulated William on the job he did.

In the summer of 1870, May and Helen participated in a hunting expedition in which May shot and slightly wounded a buffalo. The injured animal charged after the young woman while the other hunters watched in horror, unable to help her. William, who had been on a scouting trip for the army, suddenly arrived on the scene and brought the buffalo down before it reached May. Once Cody made sure his sisters were all right, he reprimanded them for leaving the fort without him. An article about the incident that appeared in an Omaha newspaper the following day incorrectly cited May as the sharpshooter who had killed the buffalo.

The exaggerated account of May's courage and ability with a gun was the inspiration for a melodrama written by E. C. Judson in 1877. William starred in *May Cody; or, Lost and Won*. One of the show's cast members was L. E. Decker. May fell in love with the handsome actor, and the two were married shortly after the premiere of the program. The play was a huge success, and, for a brief time, May enjoyed a bit of the fame that her brother had experienced.[21]

William sought advice from all his sisters about his finances, career, and romantic pursuits. Helen was the first sibling he confided in regarding his feelings for Louisa Frederici. The Civil War was close to ending, and William briefly allowed his attention to be diverted from his military assignment and long days on the trail to courtship. According to Helen, William was instantly smitten with Louisa. "From war to love, or from love to war, is but a step, and Will lost no time in taking it. He was somewhat better an apprentice to Dan Cupid. . . . His opportunities to enjoy feminine society had not been many, which, perhaps, accounts for the promptness with which he embraced them when they did arise. He became the accepted suitor of Miss Louisa Frederici before . . . his regiment was mustered out."[22]

In time, Louisa and William sent a letter to his sisters announcing their engagement. Julia quickly responded with her best wishes and hope for a happy life together. She wrote that her one regret was that their mother was not alive to share the joy.[23] "I was almost hysterical with happiness," Louisa recalled in her journal upon meeting the Cody sisters for the first time.[24] "We all love sister Lou," Julia assured William after she, Eliza, May, and Helen had gotten to know her for themselves. William's sisters hoped the news of their brother's impending wedding meant that he would be staying close to home after he was married.

In her biography Julia remembered what her relatively

self-assured brother had shared with her about the time leading up to his proposing to Louisa. "He was tongue-tied around
her and unable to convey the deep affection he had. He was
so clumsy with his words he would simply stop speaking all
together and stare off in complete silence." Louisa's reassuring smile gave him the nerve to tell her how he felt. "Louisa,"
he blurted out one evening, "I love you. . . . I love you very
much . . . and I want you to be my wife." Finally, he gave her
a chance to speak. "Billy," Louisa responded. "Billy Cody, I've
been waiting to hear these very words since the first minute
I met you. I love you, and I'll marry you whenever you want
me to."[25]

Once nineteen-year-old William had proposed to Louisa,
he was determined to find a well-paying job and set money
aside to care for his future bride. He hired on with a stageline
as a driver, earning $150 a month transporting passengers,
supplies, and payroll funds between Fort Leavenworth, Kansas, and Fort Kearney, Nebraska.

William quickly became one of the stageline's best driv-
ers. The job was fairly routine. He consistently delivered his
cargo undamaged and on time. His travels were interrupted
only once by a pair of bandits as the stagecoach was leaving
the depot at Fort Kearney. Two of the men riding in William's
vehicle looked suspicious to him. He had overheard the two
mention that they were part of a gang, and their actions made
William believe they knew that the contents of the strongbox
atop the stagecoach contained a large amount of money. He
decided to hold up the passengers before they had a chance to
do the same to him.

During a stop to check the vehicle's running gear, William
ordered the men off the stage. He leveled his revolvers at them
and demanded that they throw down their guns. He then tied
them up and put them back in the vehicle. He dropped the
would-be thieves off with the sheriff at the first stage station

and, before continuing on his way, removed the money from the strongbox and hid it inside the seat cushion.

While driving through a grove of thick timber, six armed highwaymen blocked the trail and stopped the coach. The bandits rifled through the strongbox and were furious to learn it was empty. William informed them that two passengers he was traveling with earlier in the day had already taken the treasure. The criminals rode out after the fellow gang members they believed had deceived them, and William was free to carry on. He delivered the goods intact.

William wrote his sisters and Louisa about the experience. According to Helen, Louisa quickly sent word back pleading with him to "give up the wild life he was leading, return East, and find another calling." William penned a letter to his fiancée promising her that he would quit and asked her to set a wedding date.[26]

Two

The Courtship of Louisa

———•———

*I now adored [Miss Frederici] above any other young
lady I had ever seen.*

—WILLIAM CODY (1879)

William Cody waltzed his new bride, the former Louisa
Frederici, around the floor of the dining room on board
the side-wheel steamer *Morning Star*. Several eyes watched
the attractive couple gliding from one side of the room to the
other. The newlyweds were completely absorbed in each other
and took no real notice of their surroundings. William was an
attractive but wild-looking twenty-year-old with long, brown
hair that hung over his shoulders. A little mustache and goatee clung to the upper lip and chin of his ruggedly handsome
face. His fringed buckskin-style western fashion was in direct
contrast to the other male passengers, but suited his overall
unique appearance.[1]

Louisa, whom William described as a "comely St. Louis girl
of French descent," was radiant in her evening dress of black
chambray gauze. Her dark hair was braided and pinned neatly
on top of her head, and long tendrils dangled past her neck and
ears. William proudly smiled at his charming bride. Louisa
returned the favor. In that moment they saw in each other every
positive quality and wonderful characteristic they possessed.
They saw their future as hopeful and void of complications.[2]

William met Louisa in May 1865. He was a serviceman
with the Seventh Kansas Volunteer Cavalry stationed at the

military headquarters in St. Louis, Missouri. While there, he was introduced to the young woman who would become his wife. "I became acquainted with Louisa," William wrote in his biography, "a young lady whom I greatly admired and in whose charming society I spent many a pleasant hour."[3]

Margaret Louisa Frederici was born on May 27, 1843, in Arnold, Missouri. Her father, Christopher, was a successful farmer who had immigrated to the United States from Alsace-Lorraine, France. He and his wife, Elizabeth, were a very religious couple, and their three children were educated at a convent in St. Louis.[4]

Louisa was an accomplished equestrian, and, according to William, the first time he noticed her, she was riding. He told his sister Helen that "more than once while out for a morning cantor, I noticed a young woman of attractive face and figure, who sat her horse with the grace of Diana Vernon." (Vernon was a character from a popular book at the time, *Rob Roy*. She was beautiful and an exceptional horsewoman.) Helen noted in her biography that "few things caught Will's eye more quickly than fine horsemanship." William wanted to meet Louisa, but, as none of his close friends knew her, he thought it would be impossible.[5]

Louisa's cousin, Will McDonald, eventually introduced the two. While on leave from the army in May 1865, William visited Will, who was staying at the Frederici's home. Louisa was sitting in a chair in front of a fire, engrossed in a book, when William saw her. She didn't notice that the two Wills were in the room until her cousin, a notorious prankster, pulled the chair out from under her. Louisa jumped to her feet, turned, and slapped the man behind her chair. She was mortified when she realized it wasn't her cousin she hit, but William. She apologized over and over again; each time William accepted.[6]

His forgiving spirit attracted Louisa almost as much as his appearance. She recalled in her memoirs that "William

William F. Cody as a young scout, circa 1868
Buffalo Bill Historical Center, Cody, WY, P.69.26

was tall and straight and strong, his hair was jet black, his features finely molded, and his eyes clear and sharp, determined and yet kindly, with a twinkle in them." William approved highly of Louisa as well. According to his biography, he thought she was the "handsomest, sweetest thing I'd ever seen in my life."[7]

After a brief courtship, William returned to the military post to finish his time in the army. He was dispatched to a variety of camps during his career as a soldier, and he and Louisa wrote each other often. Although the correspondences were lost somewhere in the family's multiple trips over the plains, Louisa noted in her memoirs that one of those early letters "read something like this": "My dear Lulu, I know you will forgive me for calling you this—because you will always be LuLu to me, just as I will be glad if I may always be Willie to you."

In addition to writing heartfelt letters to Louisa, William penned a few poems. Louisa couldn't always make sense of the verses, but she appreciated the effort.

While writing her biography in 1919, she recalled a poem he wrote for her that consisted of only four lines: "The blazing sun of brilliant day, may veil the light of stars above. But no amount of heavy veils can o'er deceive the eyes of love."[8]

Private Cody was discharged from the military at the end of the Civil War, after which he and Louisa were reunited. William wrote in his memoirs that he had made up his mind to "capture the heart of Miss Frederici, whom I adore above any other young lady I had ever seen." Louisa felt as strongly for William as he did for her. "The result," he later noted, "was that I obtained her consent to marry me in the near future."[9]

Louisa and William exchanged vows at her parents' home on March 6, 1866, in almost the exact spot where they had met. Many of their friends and family attended the ceremony, which ended in a prayer for a long, happy life together.

**Louisa Frederici married William F. Cody on March 6, 1866. She was
twenty-two years old.**
Buffalo Bill Historical Center, Cody, WY, P.69.795

After the wedding the pair immediately headed to the
docks to board a steamer for a trip down the river to Leavenworth, Kansas. The wedding party, including the bride's
mother and father, escorted the newlyweds to the pier. A
number of passengers waiting to get on the vessel recognized William from newspaper articles and pointed him out

to one another as he and Louisa walked by them. Not everyone behaved kindly toward him and his new wife. Some of the glares cast at William were openly hostile. Soon, friends and relatives of the Fredericis were asking Louisa's father if he knew who William really was and whether his son-in-law had any credentials.

Criminal accusations, leveled by Southern sympathizers who knew that William had fought for the North in the Civil War, filtered through the crowd and found their way to Louisa's father. The claim was that William was a "desperate outlaw, bandit, and house-burner on the frontier." Louisa's father was upset by the charges and confronted William, demanding to know if there was any truth to what was being said. William explained that their bitterness was solely a result of his position in the war. His father-in-law did not readily accept the argument and threatened to take Louisa home with him. "I besought him to leave the decision to her," William recalled in his memoirs, "and for the next ten minutes I pleaded my case with all the eloquence I could command. I was talking against odds, for my wife, as well as her parents' friends, were ardent southerners. . . . But when I put the case to her she said gamely that she had taken me for better or for worse and intended to stick to me."

Louisa was in tears by the time the steamer left St. Louis. Her parents objected to her leaving with William. She hated to defy them but felt it was what she needed to do. The dispute saddened her, and no amount of reassurance from William that she had made the right decision seemed to make a difference. "When we are among northern people I will not be regarded as such a desperate character," he told her as they headed to their stateroom.

The newlyweds' situation did not improve as the day wore on. Unfriendly eyes bore holes into William's head as the pair ate their evening meal in the dining room. Passengers huddled together whispering about the couple and pointing. When the Codys stood up to dance, many of the other travelers left the dance floor. A weeping Louisa retired early to escape the rude behavior.

After she had left their table, a kind gentleman from Indiana spoke with William about the reason for the unprovoked behavior. "To tell the truth Mr. Cody," William remembered the man saying, "these men are Missourians and say they recognize you as one of Jennison's Jayhawkers; that you were an enemy of theirs." (Jennison's Jayhawkers was a nickname for the Seventh Kansas Cavalry, commanded by Colonel Charles R. Jennison, of which William was a member.)

William discussed his role as a scout and soldier with the Union army and recounted some of the early Kansas border battles in which he and his father had played a prominent part.

The captain of the steamer had seen the way some of the passengers had behaved toward the Codys and was compelled to speak with William about the situation. "It is shameful the way these people are treating you," he confessed, "but let it pass, and when we get to Independence everything will be all right."

Louisa was still crying when William returned to their stateroom. He held her tightly and told her what the captain had said. The captain's comments provided comfort enough for her to fall asleep for a little while. William was growing increasingly agitated with the Rebels' overt intrusion on his honeymoon. According to his autobiography, he "walked the floor all night."

When the Codys emerged from their room the following morning, they were greeted with more snarls from the belligerent southerners. William threatened to get his guns and settle the matter, but Louisa talked him out of it. By midafternoon the Rebels were in a rage. The steamer docked so that the crew could gather wood, and when they left the vessel, they found themselves under fire by a party of armed men on horseback. The Missourians stood on the deck excitedly watching the action and cheering. The ship's captain quickly ordered the vehicle away from the landing before any of the gunmen could jump on board. William and Louisa were witnesses to the attack and overheard the leader of the gunmen bellow, "Where is that Kansas Jayhawker? We have come for him!"

William was furious and immediately raced to the stateroom to retrieve his revolvers. He returned to the deck carrying a gun in each hand. He strode past the mouthy Confederates, defying them to challenge him. No one said a word. William proceeded to the steward's office, where he met several men dressed in blue uniforms who had been discharged from the military. "They were traveling to Kansas, in steerage, saving their money so they might have it to invest in homes when they reached their destination," William recounted in his autobiography. "They had all heard of me, and now proposed to arm themselves and defend me should there be any further hostile demonstrations. I gladly welcomed their support, more for my wife's sake than my own."[10]

The soldiers' help was ultimately not needed. William's display of weapons had defused the situation between himself and the Missourians. It was only after things had settled down that William learned that one of the southerners had telegraphed the James and Younger brothers to let them know he was on the steamship. The outlaws were to meet the ship when it docked and capture William.

Louisa was distressed not only by the news of the elaborate attempt to kill her husband but also by the sight of William brandishing a pair of revolvers. "She was now certain that I was the bandit I had been accused of being," William later recalled. The supporters William met in the steward's office assured him that his wife would soon change her mind. "Wait till she gets among Union people," one of the men told William. "She will learn her mistake then."[11]

In an effort to help dispel any false assumptions Louisa had about her new husband, the former Union soldiers and several members of the steamer's crew organized a ball to be held in the Codys' honor. The Southern sympathizers watched in disgust as the preparations were made for the event. Fearful of retaliation, the southerners demanded that the captain of the steamship let them off at the next town. The captain refused their request.

The ball was well attended by northerners and other passengers who objected to the way William and Louisa had been unfairly treated. All of Louisa's doubts and anxieties faded as she met new friends, talked about her future with William, and danced with her husband. When the couple arrived in Leavenworth, they were greeted by several of William's friends, family, business associates, and local politicians. At a banquet the newlyweds attended that evening, Louisa threw her arms around her spouse and declared that she didn't believe him to be an outlaw. "Will's arms went about my waist and he drew me to him," Louisa recollected in her biography, "and described the future he had in mind for us." "I'm taking you into a new country, a strange country," he told her.[12]

Since their wedding, neither of them had given much thought to how rough life in the unsettled West would be for Louisa. "You're going to meet gamblers and ruffians who have killed, men who have mighty little in the world to recommend them except that they are helping to populate this country out here." Louisa remembered that she was silent for a moment after William's announcement, but then she "caught his hand in hers and pressed tight."[13]

Before William and Louisa got married, she asked him to think about finding a job close to home. She didn't want to be left alone or William to be scouting the potentially dangerous plains. After considering the hardships Louisa would be exposed to on the frontier, he reluctantly agreed.

The two decided to become innkeepers at a hotel in the Salt Creek Valley. It was the same business his mother had operated at one time. The Codys named the establishment the Golden Rule House. Not only did the hotel welcome out-of-town guests, but William's sisters Helen and Mary also occupied a room there. "I seemed to have the qualifications necessary to run a business," William recalled later in his life, "but for a man who had lived my kind of life it proved a tame employment. I found myself sighing once more for the freedom of the plains."[14]

Aware of her husband's longing, Louisa released William from his promise to settle in one place. After assuring her that he could provide for her working as a plainsman, he sold the hotel, moved his bride to Leavenworth, and traveled alone to Salina, Kansas. The Kansas Pacific Railroad was in the final stages of completion when William arrived. He planned to start his own freight service, transporting supplies to rail workers in remote areas. On his first venture out, the wagon was overrun by Indians. He escaped without injury, but his load and vehicle were lost in the attack.

He walked to Junction City, where he hoped to find a job that would help him support his family and replace his property. While he was there, he met up with Bill Hickok, a scout he'd known from his army days. Hickok was employed as a sentinel with the U.S. government and suggested that William take a job doing the same work. William's reputation, combined with Hickok's recommendation, led to his being hired to scout the territory between Fort Ellsworth and Fort Fletcher.

William wrote Louisa often during his travels. He shared with her stories about the terrain, the military posts, and the people he came in contact with, including General George Custer. He served as Custer's guide from Fort Hays, Kansas, to Fort Larned. No direct trail linked the two posts, but William forged a path through the countryside. Custer was so impressed with Cody's expertise that he promised to hire him on as a full-time scout should William ever need a job. "I think that was very nice of the general," he wrote Louisa, "and I thanked him, telling him that I was a married man now and that I always would need a job to provide for my family."[15]

Louisa wrote William about her daily routine, their home, the health and welfare of his sisters, and the impending birth of their first child. On December 16, 1866, Arta Cody was born. Several months later William was able to return for a brief visit with his wife and daughter. Seeing his child prompted him to consider less life-threatening work. He decided to enter into business with a land speculator named William Rose.

The two Wills invested in property near the spot where the Kansas Pacific Railroad was to run several miles west of Fort Hays. Their plan was to lay out a town where eager settlers could live and take advantage of this advanced form of transportation. Supplies were ordered and goods were stockpiled in anticipation of the mad rush to the area that the entrepreneurs named Rome. Once the plans for the railroad community were completed, William sent for Louisa and their daughter to come and live with him. "I was at Ellsworth to meet her when she arrived bringing the baby," he noted in his memoirs. "Besides three or four wagons, in which the supplies for Rome's new general store and furniture for the little house I had built was loaded, I had a carriage for the baby. The new town was a hundred miles west. I knew it would be a dangerous trip, as the Indians had long been troublesome along the railroad."[16]

A number of immigrants bound for the new town accompanied the Codys on the journey. William, his family, and the future residents of Rome were attacked twice along the way. Louisa was upset by the raids and with her husband as well. "Mrs. Cody asked me if I had brought her and the baby out on the plains to be killed," William lamented years later. "This is the kind of life I lead every day and get fat on it, I said. But she did not seem to think it especially congenial."[17]

Louisa and William put all their belongings away in their new home and looked forward to the town growing into a booming metropolis. Louisa was left alone quite a bit while William dealt with selling lots to various homesteaders and hunted buffalo to supply meat for the graders working on the railroad. During that time she learned to handle herself effectively against wild animals and drunken soldiers who made advances.

Before Rome had barely had a chance to get up and running, a ruthless businessman saw the town's potential and offered to partner with the two Wills. William Cody turned him down, and within three days the citizens of Rome were leaving in droves. The businessman had established a railroad town of his own called Hays City and encouraged residents to move there. The promise of employment for every man in the territory at the new site led to a mass exodus from Rome.[18]

Discouraged and broke, William left the deserted town and headed to St. Louis with his wife and child. After making sure Louisa and Arta were settled at her parents' home, he returned to the plains to hunt buffalo for the railroad. Once more, William and Louisa were separated, with only letters to connect them until he came home again.

THREE

Husband, Father, Scout, and Actor

---•---

My restless, roaming spirit would not allow me to remain at home very long.

—WILLIAM CODY (1904)

In late February 1869, Louisa and her two-year-old daughter Arta were tucked safely inside her parents' home in St. Louis, Missouri. It was cold, and she stood over a fire blazing in a grate fireplace trying to get warm. Her little girl was nearby playing on the floor with a doll. Preoccupied with rereading a letter from William, Louisa paid little attention to the knock on the front door, nor did she look up from the letter when her mother answered the door. The sound of a familiar voice booming over Elizabeth Frederici's cheerful welcome prompted Louisa to set aside the correspondence.

Arta immediately recognized the burly figure that entered the room as her father's. She hurried to William, and he scooped her into his arms. Louisa was less certain that the man was her husband. There was a long moment of silence as she studied his face and rugged manner of dress. The change in his appearance was so striking that she could only stare at him. "Where the close cropped hair had been were long, flowing curls now," she later wrote in her memoirs. "A mustache weaved its way outward from his lower lip, while a small goatee showed black and spot-like on his chin."[1]

Louisa slowly approached William and then cupped his chin in her hand. He smiled back at her, and she hugged him around the neck, stroking his matted, unruly mane. "What happened to your hair?" she asked, smoothing it down and pushing several strands behind his ear. "This is how they wear it on the plains," he replied unapologetically. "If it were any shorter I couldn't claim to be a scout." He went on to explain that any Indian who got the better of him would have quite a scalp on his hands.[2]

William pulled Louisa close to him and kissed her face. They were happy to see each other, but she thought he looked thin and tired. She promised to serve him a fine meal once he "made himself presentable." After playfully tossing his daughter in the air a few times and tickling her ribs, he reluctantly went to take a bath and change out of his buckskins into store-bought clothes.

William's appearance was significantly less wild when he sat down to eat dinner that evening with his family. It gave Louisa pleasure to see how well he liked her cooking. Still, the good food, the congenial surroundings, his wife's attentiveness, and the affection of his daughter were not enough to entice him to stay put for an extended period of time.

General Phil Sheridan, commander of the troops on the western front, needed William as a scout for the Fifth Cavalry. The outfit was being transferred from Fort Lyon, Colorado, to Fort McPherson, Nebraska. As soon as the way was made safe from assault by the Sioux, Cheyenne, Kiowa, and Arapahoe, William promised to return for Louisa and Arta and take them with him to the Northern Plains. The day he announced that he needed to be on his way, a troubled light came to Louisa's eyes, and the lines around her mouth deepened with sorrow. She worried for her husband's well-being on such a dangerous journey. She did not doubt his ability as a hunter; indeed, she had been present at numerous shooting expeditions in which William occasionally and successfully competed.

Riflemen challenged the claim that he was the best buffalo hunter in the West. Huge sums of money were offered to William to prove his talent. Hundreds of spectators would converge at the spot where the contests were held, twenty miles east of Fort Sheridan, Illinois. William and his opponents would hunt for eight hours to see who could shoot the most buffalo. William always won. Many of the Plains Indians knew of his reputation and feared him. Louisa hoped his notoriety would protect him beyond the area where he had earned his fame. Soon after William rode off to join Sheridan's troops, Louisa began packing and making arrangements to go with him when he returned.

Riding well in advance of the cavalry, William blazed a trail through treacherous, unsettled territory scanning the area for hostile Indians. Not far from Fort Larned, Kansas, where his trip originated, he spotted a large gathering of Kiowa and Comanche warriors. Other than being restless and anxious about receiving a herd of cattle the U.S. government had promised the tribes, the Indian leaders assured William that they were not planning any attack, and he accepted their word. He did not fail to notice, however, that many of the Indians were armed with rifles and had a generous supply of ammunition. He continued on his way but kept a careful eye out for tribesmen who might be considering going on the warpath.

Days after his first encounter with the Indians, he was hurrying toward the next outpost on the trek to get supplies and a fresh mount when he was stopped by forty warriors. He recognized them as the same men he had met outside Fort Larned. Their faces were now smeared with red paint, and their demeanor was clearly unfriendly. William was jerked off his ride, disarmed, and escorted to their camp along the Arkansas River. After some fast talking and the promise to help round up several head of cattle and drive them to their village, William was set free.

More than a dozen warriors trailed along behind him to make sure he would do what he said. William slowly managed to pull ahead of his followers and eventually spurred his ride into a full gallop. A chase between the scout and the Indians ensued. The warriors were gaining on William just as he spotted a party of soldiers moving out of a thicket beside a stream. The troops noticed that William was in trouble and took position with their rifles to fire on the incoming Indians. When William reached the soldiers, he leaped off his mount and fell in with them. Several shots were fired, and two Indians were killed. The remaining warriors turned away from the ambush and rode back to their encampment.[3]

The Indian uprising along the route did not end with the exchange of gunfire outside Fort Larned. Native Americans were sullen and bitter about the intrusion on their land and the slaughter of the buffalo. From the time William left Louisa at the Kansas military post in 1867 until the time he was able to move his family to Nebraska two years later, he would be involved in numerous skirmishes with a variety of Indian tribes.

One of the most dangerous of the armed conflicts occurred in the summer of 1869 on the north fork of Nebraska's Beaver Creek. William was leading a group of civilian scouts and Fifth Cavalry soldiers through this dangerous area when they happened upon a tribe of more than three hundred Cheyenne warriors and their families. All were traveling along the water's edge. Word of the Indians' presence was sent to the commander of the troops, and orders were given to the soldiers to keep themselves low in the ravine to avoid being detected. William was sent ahead to find out how quickly the Indians were moving and in what direction. He returned with the recommendation that the cavalry attack the Cheyenne before they discovered the army was there.

The tribe was not caught unaware. Their own scouts had caught sight of the army. The Indians lined up on one side of the creek bed and were waiting for the advancing soldiers. The Fifth Cavalry's commander, General Carr, divided his men into divisions and concentrated a wave of troops on the point in the line that had the fewest warriors. A rogue lieutenant decided to attack another point in the line and found himself and his division surrounded by a hundred warring Cheyenne. While the remaining troops fought to rescue the men, the Indians fortified their defense. They held off the cavalry long enough to get the women and children out of the area and then, a little at a time, began retreating toward the Republican River.

William's superior shooting and riding skills were instrumental in driving the Cheyenne into the hills and out of the immediate area. The grueling battle had left the scout and the other members of the cavalry exhausted and in need of provisions, ammunition, fresh horses, and reinforcements. The soldiers knew the Cheyenne were tenacious and would mount a counterattack. They knew they would need more help to fight back the rested warriors. William, who had been severely wounded in the episode, volunteered to travel to the nearest fort for assistance.

General Carr recalled William's brave ride in his daily log: *His head was swathed in a bloody handkerchief, which served as a bandage as well as a chapeau, his hat having been shot off, the bullet plowing his scalp badly for about five inches. He was bleeding profusely—a very close call, but a lucky one. The advance guard had been relieved, the Indians severely punished, with a loss on our side of only three killed. Our greatest need was supplies, which the hot trail had side tracked. As the country was infested with Indians, and it was fifty miles to the nearest supply point, Fort Kearney, on consultation with Cody he decided it would be best to undertake the job himself, a point of characteristic* [sic] *of him, as he never shirked duty or faltered in emergencies.*

I gave him the best horse in the outfit, and when twilight arrived, he, after patching up his head a little, was off to bring relief and meet us at a point northwest about a day's march away. These were about the most definite directions any scout got in the trackless wastes. . . . Cody made a ride of fifty miles during the night, arriving at Fort Kearney at daylight.

He had chased and fought Indians all day, been wounded, and when, through his rare frontier instinct, he reached us he had been almost constantly in the saddle and without sleep for forty hours.[4]

By late summer 1869, William had moved Louisa and Arta to Fort McPherson, and the family was busy partaking in the many social engagements at the post. At twenty-two, Buffalo Bill, as many came to call him, was recognized by military leaders and government officials as the best guide and hunter on the plains. He and Louisa were highly sought-after guests at dinners, dances, and weekly stage plays.

Female camp followers—wives and daughters of the military men stationed at the fort—found William's unconventional looks appealing. They were attentive and eager to be near him. Louisa had become accustomed to William's long whiskers and found them as attractive as the other ladies did.[5] She had her share of admirers at the post as well. Settlers, soldiers, and cowboys kept her dance card full at every gala.[6]

William was proud of his wife, and in the first year together at the army camp, the two shared many wonderful memories. Years later, Louisa fondly recalled a Christmas when William left the fort to travel to Cheyenne, Wyoming, to bring back "gifts and other necessities of the season." While waiting for him to return, she and some of the other wives decorated the

Cody family photograph—William, Louisa, and their daughter Arta,
circa 1870
Buffalo Bill Historical Center, Cody, WY, P. 69.756

hall where a Christmas party was to be held. She helped pre-
pare a massive holiday meal for the soldiers and their families
as well. William arrived back at the post with a wagon that
was overflowing with presents for Arta and the other children
who lived there. "The program," Louisa later wrote, "came off
in high style, except when our daughter stood up and recited

a bit of a silly verse her father had taught her, instead of the more appropriate recitation I had selected for her."[7]

The Codys' home at Fort McPherson was a modest two-room cabin with an adjacent small log barn. Before Louisa and Arta's arrival, William had furnished the home with items he had ordered from a store in Cheyenne. In his attempt to make the primitive structure presentable for his wife and child, he tried to paper the rough walls of the cabin. He abandoned the chore before it was completed. "I'm more of a success as an Injun killer," he told his wife as she inspected the messy job. Louisa was grateful for her husband's efforts.[8]

William wasn't the only one in the family who had dangerous dealings with the Native Americans who surrounded the post. Louisa had her share of menacing encounters as well. One incident occurred at the Codys' cabin while Louisa and her friend, Mrs. Charles McDonald, were working on sewing projects. They heard a noise outside the building and spotted hostile Indians lurking about. The two women knew that Indian warriors were mortally afraid of drunken women, so the pair guzzled down a bottle of tea and pretended to be inebriated. When the Indians saw their behavior, they fled in terror. William was pleased with the fact that Louisa could take care of herself if needed. He didn't worry too much about the safety of his wife and baby when he was out on a scouting mission because he knew she was a capable woman.

The Codys' marriage grew strong during their time at the fort. The time they spent together during breaks between scouting expeditions and community activities was enjoyable. They looked forward to the arrival of a baby and building a life for themselves in Nebraska once William's commitment to the army reached its end. Louisa had big plans for herself and her husband, but so did Ned Buntline.

Ned Buntline was a newspaper publisher and writer. He was traveling through the region delivering lectures on the

evils of drinking when he met William. The two men met each
other at Fort Sedgwick, Nebraska. Ned was fascinated with
the adventures the seasoned scout had experienced. He spent
hours questioning William about his life and listening to har-
rowing tales of near-death experiences and survival on the
untamed frontier. Ned was so impressed with William that
when he returned to his home state of New York, he penned a
dime novel entitled *Buffalo Bill: The King of Bordermen—the
Wildest and Truest Story I Ever Wrote.*[9]

The book was a huge success and helped make William
the most famous westerner to date. The book became a series,
and William read each installment with great enthusiasm
and wonder. He and Ned corresponded between novels, and
any new stories involving the daring scout's encounters with
Indians were transformed into another book.[10]

William's popularity was still on the rise when his and Louisa's son was born on November 26, 1870. The couple named
him Kit Carson, after the famed frontiersman William had
met when he was a boy. Not long after Kit's birth, William was
offered the job of justice of the peace of Cottonwood Springs.
The onetime Pony Express station and county seat for North
Platte was one mile southeast of Fort McPherson. A series of
crimes were being perpetrated outside the jurisdiction of the
post. Government property was being hijacked coming into and
going out of the army camp. Because the post commander had
no jurisdiction over the civilians who were behind the thefts, a
judge to handle such legal issues had to be appointed.

At first, William was hesitant about accepting the job. He
told the post commander that he didn't "know any more about
law than a government mule does about book-keeping."[11] Believing the job would not only keep William close to her but also be
a prestigious honor, Louisa convinced him to take the position.
William tracked down horse thieves, settled property disputes,
officiated at weddings, and presided over divorce proceedings.[12]

KIT CARSON CODY

The Codys' only son, Kit Carson Cody, born at Fort McPherson, Nebraska (1870)
Buffalo Bill Historical Center, Cody, WY, P.69.194

William's interest in scouting and buffalo hunting did not wane with his new position. He was called on many times to guide buffalo-hunting parties for such well-known men as General Phil Sheridan and the grand duke of Russia. Louisa sent her husband out on such expeditions dressed in elaborate, ornamental garments she had stitched herself. Those who accompanied him on various hunts wrote about how striking William looked. For example, General Henry E. Davies made this observation: "Tall and somewhat slight in figure, though possessed of great strength and iron endurance, straight and erect as an arrow, and with strikingly handsome features, he once attracted to him all with whom he became acquainted, and the better knowledge we gained of him during the days he spent with our party increased the good impression he made upon his introduction."[13]

The hunting parties William organized and led earned him a considerable amount of money as well as gifts of furs and priceless jewels. He was mindful of providing for his family's well-being but was prone to mismanaging his income if Louisa did not intercede. He was overly generous to his friends and made poor investment decisions. Louisa was thrifty and, although she liked fine things, lived in moderation.

The buffalo hunt William planned for Russia's Grand Duke Alexis resulted in not only a substantial fee for his work but also a trip to New York. William had always wanted to visit the East Coast, and out of gratitude for the excellent entertainment Cody had provided, the duke made arrangements for the scout to make the journey.

Had it not been for the fact that Louisa was expecting their third child, she would have accompanied William on the excursion. Nonetheless, she made sure that her husband was ready for his introduction into eastern society. She worked diligently on adding appropriate garments to his wardrobe. "We procured some blue cloth at the commissary and, sewing day and night, I made Will his first real soldier suit," Louisa recalled in her memoirs, "with a Colonel's gold braid on it, with stripes and cords and all the other gingerbread of an old-fashioned suit of blues."[14] ("Colonel" was an honorary title that the governor of Nebraska had given to William while serving in the Nebraska National Guard.)

William was well received at every stop along the tour of the eastern cities. He was treated to fine meals with high-ranking government officials and well-known entertainers.

He was invited to balls and introduced to troupes of beautiful women, all seeking his favor and attention. Journalists followed William everywhere he went and recorded what he said at the many events he attended, including a performance of a play written by Ned Buntline based on the novel the author had penned about the daring scout.

The audience gave William a standing ovation when they were informed he was in the theater. At Ned's insistence, he reluctantly made his way to the center of the stage to take a bow. The response prompted the backers of the show to offer William $500 to play himself. "You might as well try to make an actor out of a government mule," William told the theater manager.[15]

William extended his trip by ten days and would have continued traveling a bit longer if not for an order from General Sheridan to return to Fort McPherson. Before being rushed off to another uprising between the army and the Indians, he enjoyed a brief visit with his wife and children. He shared the particulars of his trip with Louisa but chose not to elaborate on the ladies he met at the various dances where he was a guest. She learned the details of those outings on her own through the newspaper accounts of his journey.

William wasn't home long before he was hired on as a scout with another hunting expedition. The time he spent in New York away from the job had made him feel a little insecure about whether he could still do the work. "Why, Mamma," he joked to Louisa, "I'm such a tenderfoot right now from being away that I'd run if I even saw an Injun!"[16]

In spite of his brief doubts, he proved himself on the wild plains again and again. In the summer of 1872, he and his scouting partner, Texas Jack Omohundro, led a group of British sportsmen on a hunting trip that was attacked by North Platte Indians. Not only did William protect the sportsmen from being killed or captured, but he also helped them acquire the buffalo they hoped to win. William's contribution as a scout for the military, combined with his work in helping to keep the peace on the wild frontier, was recognized by the U.S. government when it presented him with the Congressional Medal of Honor.

In between the various hunting trips, military assignments, award ceremonies, and a short-lived stint in politics, William became a father for the third time. Louisa gave birth to Orra Maude on August 13, 1872. Not long after the baby was born, Louisa's parents urged her to bring the children to St. Louis for a visit, and she agreed.

While his family was away, William decided to accept Ned's persistent requests to travel with him to Chicago and appear as the lead in the stage play about Cody's adventures. William wrote Louisa of his intentions, noting, "I don't know just how bad I'd be at actin'. I guess maybe I better find out."[17]

Ned assumed William would make the trip to Illinois with a troupe of westerners in tow (Indians, trappers, riders, and so on) who would participate in the show with him. Texas Jack was the only person with him when he arrived in Chicago. Ned was so excited that William had changed his mind about participating in the play that he wasn't overly concerned about the additional casting. However, the owner of the theater where the program was to take place was furious—not only because William came to town with just one other person but also because the play itself hadn't been written yet.

The situation was quickly remedied. Ned penned a melodrama entitled *The Scouts of the Prairie*; actors, dancers, and set builders were hired. All those who hadn't answered the call to go west were invited to see the play depicting the wilds beyond the Rockies. On December 12, 1872, audiences flocked to the opening-night performance. The box-office receipts for the debut show were more than $2,800. Ned took his troupe of novice entertainers on the road. Despite the poor reviews the

Arta, William F., Louisa, and Orra Cody, circa 1880
Buffalo Bill Historical Center, Cody, WY, P.6.813

show received for its writing and some of the performances, *The Scouts of the Prairie* was a financial success.

Louisa was taken aback when William announced he was going to resign as a scout for the army so that he might continue with Ned's show. "His primary motivation was providing for the children," Louisa wrote in her memoirs. "He wanted money to send the children to fine schools and give them everything they needed."[18] By the end of the first season, William had earned more than $6,000. It was more money than he had made in all the years he had been a military scout.

His family accompanied him on the road until he purchased a home for them in Rochester, New York, in mid-1873. After making sure Louisa and the children had all they would need until he could see them again, he rode off to rejoin the cast of Ned's show and enjoy the additional fame the play offered him. He would be on the road for the next three years.

FOUR

Life in the Limelight

---•---

Your third child will be a boy. You should give him the world. He will be famous. His name will be known to all—young and old, rich and poor. People will love and praise him. He may even be president of the United States.

—GYPSY SEERESS'S PREDICTION FOR MARY LAYCOCK CODY, BUFFALO BILL'S MOTHER (1839)

William stared down at a blank piece of paper desperately trying to find the words to describe the devastating circumstances surrounding his family in the spring of 1876. He glanced over at Louisa, stretched out on one of the beds in his daughter's room at their home in Rochester, New York. For days she had been caring for their three children, all of whom had come down with scarlet fever. The highly contagious illness had forced the youngsters to struggle with acute abdominal pains, sore throats, vomiting, and a rash. The Codys' eight-year-old daughter Arta and three-year-old Orra were over the worst of the sickness, but five-year-old Kit never recovered. The Codys were crushed.

William had been onstage performing in *The Scouts of the Plains* in Springfield, Massachusetts, when a telegram from Louisa arrived, informing him that Kit was dying. He left the theater after the first act of the show and made a mad dash home. When William arrived at his son's bedside, Kit was drenched with sweat from a fever and in a weakened state but managed to embrace his father. Less than twenty-four hours later, the boy passed away.

Overwhelmed by the tragedy, William could neither sleep nor bring himself to share the sad news with his sisters. As he watched his wife and two girls sleeping, he reflected on Kit's short life and the joy he had brought his parents. According to Helen Cody Wetmore, "Kit was a handsome boy, with striking features and curly hair." Louisa always dressed him in the finest clothes. He was so adorable that gypsies had carried him away the previous summer. The worrisome incident helped prove that Kit was just as clever as he was handsome. After being kidnapped, he marked the trail the gypsies traveled and was able to find his way home using the noted path.[1]

Kit often visited the theaters where William was working. "He watched the seats fill in keen anxiety," Helen recalled in her memoirs, "and the moment the curtain rose and his father appeared on the stage, he would make a trumpet of his little hands, and shout from his box, 'Good house, Papa!'"[2]

Somewhere before dawn after Kit "fell asleep," as William described it, Cody wrote his sister Julia about what had happened:

April 22, 1876. To my oldest sister Julia, You are the first to write to after our sad, sad loss. Julia, God has taken from us our only little boy. He was too good for this world. We loved him too dearly he could not stay. God wanted him where he could live in a better world. So he sent an Angel of death to take the treasure that he had given us five years and five months ago. And how dear he had grown to us in that time. And when we seen that there was danger of him leaving us how we all clung to him and prayed God not to take him from us our little boy. . . . The messenger seems not to have been satisfied by plucking the brightest, brightest flower

and is still hovering near by thinking whether he
shall take the others or not. . . . Lulu is worn out
and sick. It is now three o'clock in the morning. I
must write to Lida [a nickname for Eliza], Nellie &
May. Goodbye from Brother Will.[3]

On April 24, 1876, Louisa and William buried their son at Mount Hope Cemetery, not far from their New York home. William tried to comfort himself and his wife with the sentiment that Kit "has joined the innumerable company of the white-souled throng in the regions of the blest."[4]

William had a limited amount of time to be with Louisa and his daughters after they buried Kit. The theatrical season needed to be completed, and obligations to his partners in the Buffalo Bill Combination had to be fulfilled. The Buffalo Bill Combination was the name given to the troupe of trick shooters, riders, and performers that had been assembled. The troupe was scheduled to appear in theaters throughout the mid-west during the spring that Cody's son died. William stayed with his family until the girls had fully recovered and then reluctantly returned to the show. Not wanting to burden Louisa with his grief, he shared his heartache mainly with Julia. According to the biography Julia penned about her brother, Kit's death had a profound effect on William. "On stage he was dashing, fearless and most effective," she wrote, "but [after his son died] the thrill of trouping was gone."[5]

If William's heart was not fully in his work, Louisa imagined he would find relief in the arms of one of the many enamored female theatergoers or a cast member. Rumors about William's overly attentive female fans and coworkers had reached her, and she was hurt and jealous. Before relinquishing his duties with the army, William was never at home for more than six consecutive months at a time. Now that he was an actor, the time had lessened considerably. Louisa's insecurities about their marriage and her suspicion that William was being unfaithful grew the longer he was away. Years later, Louisa told newspaper reporters that William was "immoral with every woman he met while traveling."[6]

Given the problems at home, many of William's friends and family members questioned his decision to take the show to more cities across the country. Louisa would have preferred a more stable and prestigious line of work for him and suggested he go into politics. "Mama," William told his wife, "I know I'd be a fizzle at legislatin'."[7]

His sisters, particularly Julia, were supportive of his career choice. Since premiering in Ned Buntline's *Scouts of the Prairie* with fellow scout Texas Jack Omohundro, William had become an accomplished entertainer. From the beginning of his theatrical venture, Julia had written her brother letters of encouragement. He was always quick to respond, sharing with her news about the various places he visited and the people he met:

May 11, 1873. My Dear Sister . . . I was ever so glad to hear from you and to hear you are all well. Lulu has not been well for some time, but she is getting better. . . . We have about 17 hundred relations living near Philadelphia. We had a family dinner while in Philadelphia and there were 42 persons to dine all uncles, aunts, cousins, half cousins and so forth. They are all nice good people they liked to talk me to death about our family. When I get rich I will have you all come and see them—I was going to send some presents to you all but Lulu said she knowed what to buy better than me so I left her to do it. I will surely pay you a visit this summer as I am going to go to Nebraska for a hunt this summer I will probably go to Europe this fall. . . . Love to all, Your Affectionate Brother, Will.[8]

William at age sixty-one with his sisters in 1907. Julia, age sixty-four, is seated on his right; Helen, age fifty-six, on his left; and May, age fifty-four, is in the middle.
Buffalo Bill Historical Center, Cody, WY, P.6.537.2

William's first theatrical season came to a close in June 1873. After taking care of his wife and children, he shared his profits with other family members. Although Louisa doubted that William had been faithful to her, she was appreciative that he had provided a more comfortable life for her and their children. She was pleased with their new home in New York and all the other luxuries they now could afford. "Unheard extravagances became ours," she wrote in her biography. "And Will, dear, generous soul that he was, believed that an inexhaustible supply of wealth had become his forever."[9]

If Louisa thought that the house in Rochester would provide William with an incentive to stay home, her hopes were quickly dashed. In addition to performing in a new theatrical production and organizing hunting parties, William led an army expedition through the Bighorn Mountains and aided soldiers in ushering renegade Indians back onto designated reservations. In between each venture, he returned to New York. He cherished the time he spent with his children but did not relish the disagreements he had with Louisa over his long absences.

"Our dispositions were not such as to get along well together," William confessed years later. "And I knew the longer I staid [*sic*] we were likely to grow into more trouble or something of that kind."[10] Among the many things that William thought displeased Louisa was his attachment to his sisters. He felt she resented them and their many visits to see him. "There seemed to be some friction in the family," he recalled in 1904, "and she [Louisa] naturally complained of what appeared to me was fault-finding without a cause when I was doing the best I could. . . . It kind o' grated on my nerves and I would pull out to the plains again."[11]

William took to the plains after a directive from the U.S. Army advised him that his scouting services were desperately needed in the Dakotas. Upset about the many broken promises made to them, the Cheyenne and Sioux Indians in the

Black Hills area had planned to go to war together against the U.S. government. They vowed to stop white settlers arriving on their land. General George Custer and his men had already suffered a major defeat against the Indians at the battle of Little Bighorn, and tensions were running high.

Not long after that conflict, William and the Fifth Cavalry met eight hundred Cheyenne warriors and their chief, Yellow Hand (also known as Yellow Hair), in a heated engagement late in the summer of 1876. The Indians were pushed onto a reservation, ending the uprising in the process. As always, William first shared the news of his exploits with the one person he was closest to, Julia:

> *September 4, 1876. My Dear Sister—you no doubt will be surprised to hear from me away up in this country. I'm sure you heard I have gone back to my old life that of a scout. Well so I did. I could not remain east while this Indian war was going on without taking up a hand. . . . I would have come by and seen you but the government was hurrying me up so I could not find time. I did not have time to go to Denver and see Nellie and May. So Ed brought them over to Cheyenne since then I have been continually in the saddle. I have been in several fights and killed 3 Indians during the summer I call my own. That is I never say that I kill an Indian without I get his scalp. I sent two scalps east . . . and I have one on the boat with me that I killed one week ago yesterday.*
>
> *My wound is but a slight one. [He suffered an injury in a fight with Yellow Hand and his men on July 17, 1876.] Two weeks at home will fix me all right. Then I am perfect to return to my command.*[12]

William eventually wrote to Louisa and explained the brutal encounter he had had with the Cheyenne chief. She had not heard from him in some time and was worried about his well-being. "I daily lived in hopes of a letter from him," she noted in her memoirs, "and in dread of bad news from some other source." The letter she finally received from William was enclosed in a package that contained a disturbing item. "I pried open the lid," Louisa later wrote, "and a very unpleasant odor caught my nostrils. I reeled slightly, reached for the contents, and then fainted. For I had brought from the box the scalp of an Indian." William later informed her that the scalp belonged to Yellow Hand. Louisa listened in horror as he described the fight between him and the Indian. Thoroughly disgusted by the barbaric behavior, she made William promise that he would never scalp another Indian. He was making plans for another theatrical production that focused on the scalping when he agreed.[13]

William's battle with the Cheyenne, including his duel with Yellow Hand, was a widely publicized event. Writer and actor J. V. Arlington transformed the heated confrontation into a five-act play. The drama also included a reenactment of Custer's Last Stand. William was quickly hired to portray not only himself but also Custer onstage. The play, entitled *The Red Right Hand; or Buffalo Bill's First Scalp for Custer*, opened to rave reviews in Rochester and New York City. The next stop on the tour was California.

The idea that William was going to be leaving home again annoyed Louisa. The two argued, and Louisa told William that she was taking the children and moving back to her parents' home in Missouri. According to a court deposition William gave in 1904, he could not persuade her otherwise. "I divided what money I had with her and she went to St. Louis. I went on to California." En route to the West Coast, William invested in a land and cattle venture in Nebraska and purchased several thousand acres in the Bighorn Basin of Wyoming.[14]

By the time William arrived at the Bush Theatre in San Francisco, where his show was being held, the theater was sold out. For several nights he played to a standing-room-only crowd. His success as a showman was growing, but he missed his family. A letter from his sister May indicated that Louisa had had a change of heart. She had visited her sister-in-law in Colorado and poured her feelings out to her about the fight she and William had. She was sorry for her part in their disagreement and wanted William to come back to her. "My sister begged me in her letter to do so," William recalled in 1904. "I finally consented and I went to Denver and at my sister's house I again met her [Louisa] and as she said she was sorry for what she had done we concluded to try again."[15]

Louisa and William tried to patch up their differences on a new ranch house in North Platte. William spared no expense in the construction of the magnificent home, which was built on property he had previously purchased. Lumber for the structure, which Louisa referred to as "a little less than a mansion," was carted in from Vermont, and the interior was decorated with furniture from Chicago and New York. William remained at home for several months, tending to his livestock, playing with his children, and taking long rides with Louisa along the Dismal River. For a while the couple was content. "We had money now, plenty of it," Louisa wrote in her memoirs about their life in Nebraska. "All about us ranchers were beginning to take up their claims and begin the life that Will had always dreamed. . . . The untrammeled 'great American desert' was beginning to fade forever."[16]

During the summer months of 1879, 1880, and 1882, William shared a career goal with Louisa that he believed would delight them both for the rest of their lives. "It will take a lot of planning and a lot of money," Louisa remembered her husband saying. "William's fondest ambition, outside of living a life in the 'bright, free sunshine of the west,'" she added in her autobiography, "was creating a massive western show."

"All the people back east want to find out just what the west looks like," William told Louisa, "and you can't tell them on a stage. There ain't no room. So why not take the west right to them?" He explained his elaborate plans to his interested wife. He wanted to transport the prairie, Indians, buffalo, horses, and stagecoaches by train to the East Coast and beyond. Louisa remembered the two talking for hours about the grand project, "like two enthusiastic, happy children planning a 'play show' in the back yard."[17]

William invested countless hours in organizing a Wild West program. He made plans to recruit Native Americans, trick ropers, riders, and sharpshooters. Numerous guests arrived at the ranch to help plan the show. Numerous guests, including William's theatrical associates and their children, arrived at the ranch to help plan the show. Louisa, who was feeling pushed aside by then, had limited tolerance for the frequent barrage of out-of-towners. At times she was sullen and withdrawn.[18]

Despite what William referred to as her "depressing conduct," Louisa did attend the opening performance of his new show in the fall of 1876.[19] The show, entitled *The Mountain Meadow Massacre*, debuted at the Baltimore Opera House. William was well received by audiences from Rochester to Omaha and had the attention of many women. Their constant presence unnerved Louisa. At the conclusion of the theatrical season, she witnessed four actresses—Ada Forester, Connie Thompson, Tillie Shields, and Liddy Denia—kissing William. Louisa misinterpreted the friendly gesture, and the argument that ensued between her and William was a heated one.[20]

Louisa kept a close eye on William and the attentive ladies who were involved with his 1878–1879 show *The Knight of the Plains*. He found such close scrutiny and the complaining that went along with it distracting. It had a definite effect on his job. When Louisa decided to return to the ranch in Nebraska in February 1878, William was glad to see her go. "It [Louisa's behavior] kept me disturbed and made me nervous," he revealed in 1904. "I was doing a very particular act in the way of shooting that when I would get excited and nervous over these family jars, I wasn't in a fit condition to do justice to my performances."[21]

William's autobiography, *William F. Cody as Buffalo Bill the Famous Hunter*, released in 1879, did little to help alleviate Louisa's jealousy or lessen her complaints. He made mention of the "throngs of beautiful ladies" around him and how embarrassed he was by their attention; however, he was not shy about being photographed with the women. He posed for many pictures with female followers. Even pen-and-ink artists captured the showman's image on canvas with genteel fans on his arm.

Although his amiable, sometimes flirtatious personality kept him at odds with Louisa, he did appreciate seeing her happy and attempted to make her happy whenever he could. The house they built in Nebraska seemed to make up for some of his shortcomings. "One great source of pleasure to me was that my wife was delighted with the home I had given her and the prairies of the far west," William recalled in his memoirs.[22]

For years William dutifully sent a large portion of the money he earned performing to the Codys' bank account in North Platte. He hoped that Louisa would recognize his fiscal faithfulness and that the monetary security he provided would make her just as happy as their home. As always, some of the income went to support his family, Louisa's parents, and his sisters. Now he was also providing for upkeep of the ranch and the purchase of additional acreage. In addition, some of the funds were to be used to help finance the lavish Wild West show William had dreams of producing. He believed that Louisa wanted to see his dream realized just as much as he did. When he learned that the deed to the land he thought he co-owned with Louisa did not have his name on it, he was stunned.

In March 1882 he expressed his irritation over the matter in a letter to Julia. With no land to borrow against to finance the bulk of the Wild West show, William felt that his dream might not be realized:

> *My Dear Sister, I am in a peck of trouble. What do you think? Lulu has got most if not all of our North Platte property in her name. Now what do you think of that? Ain't that a nice way for a wife to act? . . . Would you have thought that of Lulu? After all these years of my working for her. I don't care a snap for the money, but the way she has treated me.*[23]

Louisa did not consider whether William might see her actions as a betrayal. She believed she was protecting her long-term interests and those of her children from an overly ambitious spouse who might possibly risk everything to fund a theatrical production. In her opinion she was a dutiful wife who was exercising good business sense. The couple did not speak to each other for some time over the incident.[24]

The setback did not stop William from continuing to organize the Wild West show. He was certain it would be professionally satisfying and would also bring in the money he would need to build a house for himself.

By the summer of 1882, the Codys were once again civil to each other and were preparing to spend the Fourth of July with the citizens of North Platte. The townspeople had asked William to participate in the Independence Day celebration, and he decided to present a portion of the western show he had been working on and rehearsing. The production featured expert riders demonstrating how to lasso and brand cattle, how to break a wild stallion, and how to hunt and shoot buffalo. The "Old Glory Blowout," as it came to be known, was the most popular and well-attended event in the county's history. The enthusiastic reception the program received gave William the incentive he needed to take the show on the road.

Two months before William escorted his crew out of North Platte, Louisa gave birth to their third daughter. Irma Louise was born on February 9, 1883. William proudly carried his baby around for all the cast members to see.

Buffalo Bill's Wild West show opened in Omaha on May 17, 1883. His partner in the venture was Nate Salsbury. Salsbury's background was in theatrical presentations. He was also a performer and co-creator of the frontier review William had initially conceived. With the assistance of publicist John Burke, fifty cowboys, a large company of Indians, Mexican vaqueros, bucking horses, and a herd of buffalo, the troupe prepared to dazzle audiences.[25]

Louisa attended the show's debut in Chicago, the next stop on the tour after Omaha. She and William both felt that success there meant the world. "Our every cent was in that show," Louisa recalled years later. It cost thousands and thousands to purchase the equipment, to hire the actors, and to transport the big organization across the country. Other thousands were tied up in printing and the salaries of men going on in advance to make the arrangements for the show's coming. And if we failed we knew that failure would follow us everywhere."[26]

William and Louisa were anxious about whether there would be an audience for the event. Their concerns were laid to rest once they learned that every seat in the house had been sold out. William's first entrance brought sustained cheers and applause. "Time after time Will was called forth, mounted on his big, sleek horse, to receive the approval of the tremendous crowds," Louisa noted in her biography. "There was no worriment after that—our fortunes were made."[27]

Neither the elation over the initial success of the show nor the children they shared could make the Codys any better suited for each other. Adding to the strain in their

Orra Maude Cody was born in 1872. Her death in October 1883, at the age of ten, was a devastating loss for her parents.
Buffalo Bill Historical Center, Cody, WY, P.69.272

marriage was the fact that their ten-year-old daughter Orra was sickly and their oldest child, Arta, was away at boarding school and refused to answer her father's letters. William suspected that Louisa had helped drive a wedge between the two. By September 1883 William wanted out of the marriage again and was writing Julia about his intentions. "I am working my way home or at least west," he told her. "Will close in Omaha in October. Well, I have got out my petition for divorce with that woman. . . . She has tried to ruin me financially. . . . Oh I could tell you lots of funny things how she has tried to bust up the horse ranch and buy more property. I get the deeds in her name."[28]

Before William had a chance to fully act on his decision to file for divorce, Orra died in October 1883. The tragedy temporarily improved the situation between Louisa and William. They buried their daughter at the same cemetery in New York where Kit was laid to rest.

It was with a heavy heart that William rejoined the Wild West troupe to complete the theatrical season, and the remainder of the year was fraught with problems. The riverboat used to haul the show down the Mississippi crashed into another vessel, a mishap that eventually prevented the program from going on. A valued cast member died from injuries sustained in the accident as well.[29]

William survived the trying times of the 1884 season with great help from his sisters. They encouraged him to continue on and showered him with praise for his perseverance. Helen bragged about his strength of character in her 1899 biography. "Buffalo Bill . . . enters under the flash of the limelight, and sweeping off his sombrero, holds his head high, and with a ring of pride in his voice, advances before his great audience," she wrote. "He sits his horse with a natural grace much better suited to the saddle than to the Presidential chair."[30]

FIVE

The Dear Favorite

———•———

Women on the plains have prayed for him, have called
that name as the one thing between them and suicide.
—CHAUNCEY THOMAS, OUTDOOR LIFE MAGAZINE, ABOUT
WILLIAM CODY (1917)

Mollie Moses, a disheveled woman in her mid-forties, sat alone in her run-down Kentucky home, crying. She wiped her eyes with the hem of her tattered black dress and glanced up at a portrait of William Cody hanging over a cold fireplace. On the dusty coffee table in front of her lay a number of letters carefully bound together with faded ribbon. The woman's feeble finger loosened the tie and slowly unfolded one of the correspondences. Tears slid down her cheeks as she read aloud:

My Dear Little Favorite . . . I know if I had a dear little someone whom you can guess, to play and sing for me it would drive away the blues who knows but what some day I may have her eh! . . . I am not very well, have a very bad cold and I have ever so much to do. With love and kiss to my little girl—From her big boy, Bill.[1]

Mollie closed her eyes and pressed the letter to her chest, remembering. From the moment she first saw Buffalo Bill Cody at a Wild West performance, she had been captivated by him. He was fascinating—a scout, hunter, soldier, showman, and rancher. Mollie was swept away by his accomplishments, reputation, and physical stature. In September 1885 the enamored young woman from Morganfield, Kentucky, set about to win the heart of the most colorful figure of the era.[2]

William was receptive to Molly's pursuit. His all-too-frequent absences from home continued to add to the trouble he had with his wife. Louisa was critical of his actions and demanding of his time. The more she complained about the escalation in his drinking as well as his inability to manage their finances, the more distance he sought to put between them. The deaths of two of their four children, Kit in 1876 and Orra in 1883, had further strained their relationship. Louisa resented William for not being around more to help care for their children, and William was offended that she was using the funds he sent home to support his family for buying property in North Platte solely in her name.[3]

William contemplated divorce in September 1883 but reconsidered the severe act after Orra died the following month. The Codys were cordial to each other, but the marriage was void of romance. William was preoccupied with the development of the Wild West show, which he hoped to take on a multicity tour in late 1885. The undertaking was hugely expensive, and Louisa was concerned about the debts they were amassing. William predicted that the show, which would feature Annie Oakley and the famous Indian scout Sitting Bull, would leave them financially sound. The outlook on his relationship with Louisa wasn't as hopeful.[4]

Buffalo Bill was hundreds of miles from home and emotionally vulnerable when he met Mollie Moses in November 1885. She had attended one of the opening performances of the Wild West show in Shawnee Town, Illinois, and introduced herself to the star. She was an attractive widow, intelligent and sophisticated. Their encounter left a lasting impression on William, and they made arrangements to meet the following evening. Time and propriety kept them from seeing each other again before he left the area. Mollie sent William a letter expressing her delight in having made his acquaintance.

The letter she wrote to William in early November 1885 reflected her maturity and sincere interest in him. Her correspondence read like that of an experienced woman, not a lovestruck girl. The death of her husband and only child many years prior had transformed the once impetuous girl into a driven, determined woman. Mollie was educated and well-read as well as an accomplished artist and seamstress.[5]

William found those aspects of her character appealing. On November 11, 1885, he responded to her letter, forwarding his itinerary to her as well as his hope that they could meet in the future.

> *Your kind letter received. Also the beautiful little flag which I will keep and carry as my mascot, and every day I wave it to my audiences I will think of the fair donor. I tried to find you after the performances yesterday for I really wished to see you again. . . . It is impossible for me to visit you at your home much as I would like to have done so. Many thanks for the very kind invitation. I really hope we'll meet again. Do you anticipate visiting the World's Fair at New Orleans if you do will you please let me know when you are there. . . . Enclosed please find my route. I remain yours.*[6]

As the romance between Mollie and William blossomed, she expressed concerns about Louisa. In one of William's letters to Mollie, he tried to put her mind at ease on the subject.

> *My Dear Little Favorite . . . Now don't fear about my better half. I will tell you a secret. My better half and I have separated. Someday I will tell you all about it. Now do you think any the less of me? I wish I had time to write you a long letter to answer all your*

questions and tell you of myself, but I have not the
time and perhaps it might not interest you. . . . With
love and a kiss to my little girl from her big boy.[7]

Hero worship and love flared into a twin flame in Mollie's heart. She ached to be with William, and when she wasn't able to be with him at various stops on the tour, she extended invitations for him to visit her at her home. Managing the Wild West show demanded a lot of his time, and he was unable to get away as often as Mollie hoped.

My Dear . . . You say you are not my little favor-
ite or I would take the time to come to see you. My
dear don't you know that it is impossible for me to
leave my show. My expenses are $1,000 a day and
I can't. I would come if it were possible and I can't
say when I can come either but I hope to some day.[8]

William could not break free from his business, but Mollie persisted. She requested that some of his personal mementos be sent in his stead. "If you cannot be, I must have something of you near me," she wrote him. In April 1886 he answered her letter: "My Dear Little Favorite . . . Don't fear I will send a locket and picture soon. Little Pet, it's impossible for me to write from every place. I have so much to do, but will think of you from every place. Will that do? With Fond Love . . . Will."[9]

In spite of his constant reassuring, Mollie was not convinced that William and his wife were destined for divorce. When it became clear to her that William could not, or would not, fully commit to her, she requested a spot in his show. She reasoned that this was the only way she would be able to be with him all the time. Mollie was not without talent. She was a fine horsewoman and that, along with her romantic involvement with William, helped persuade him to invite her to join his troupe.[10]

Mollie and Buffalo Bill were to meet in St. Louis, a scheduled stop for the show. She was to come on board as a per-

Buffalo Bill surveys the guests at a picnic in Nebraska where many of the female attendees had jockeyed for a spot nearest the showman, circa 1878.
Buffalo Bill Historical Center, Cody, WY, P.69.983

former at that time. In an effort to make her feel welcome and show his affection, William purchased his lover a horse. The act endeared him to her even more.

> *My Dear Mollie . . . I presume you are getting about ready to come to St. Louis. Wish you would start from home in time to arrive in St. Louis about the 2nd or 3rd of May. Go to the St. James Hotel if I ain't there to meet you. I will be there any how by the 3rd. I have got you the white horse and a fine silver saddle. Suppose you have your habit. Will be glad to see you. With love, W.F.C.*[11]

Mollie's days with the Wild West show were difficult. Adapting to the rigorous traveling schedule was hard to get used to, and riding her horse day after day left her stiff and sore. Eventually Mollie lost interest in the famous program and tired of trying to win over the heart of its general manager. One of the last letters she ever received from the famous scout convinced her that the timing wasn't right for a permanent romance.

> *I have two little girls living and have lost a little boy. My wife and I have separated but are not divorced yet. That's what I meant by saying I am not yet a single man. No, dear, I'm not afraid to trust you with my secrets. You know all my family affairs. Little Pet, don't think I've forgotten you if I don't write oftener. I will write you whenever I can. With fond love, Will.*[12]

Mollie Moses returned to her home in Kentucky, where she fell into a life of poverty. She was forced to sell many of the mementos William gave her and live off the generosity of strangers in order to buy food. The two souvenirs she would never part with were the silver saddle and William's picture. Historians speculate that the demise of her relationship with Buffalo Bill left her despondent and without a will to live.

Within a few years of her parting with William, Mollie's financial situation plummeted, and she was living in squalorlike conditions. Rodents shared her house with her—rats she called her pets. One evening her "pets" bit her severely, causing her to become ill. She eventually died of complications from the bites. She was forty-three years old.[13]

Six

Away from Home

No one wants to do right more than I do and I propose
to lead an honest life.

—WILLIAM F. CODY (1901)

A petite, young reporter sat across from Buffalo Bill Cody
in his dressing room on the grounds of Ambrose Park in
Brooklyn, New York. She was mesmerized by his confident
demeanor and well-groomed look. The shock of long hair under
the enormous hat on his head was neatly coiffed, and the sig-
nature leather boots that extended to his knees were polished
black. He was a formidable man with a disarming smile that
might have put the woman at ease had she not been so star-
struck. She jotted down key points in the exclusive interview
he had granted the newspaper where she worked. The article
ran in the *New York Recorder* on May 22, 1894, and empha-
sized the progressive attitude William had toward women's
roles in society.

As the only boy in a family of five, he had personal experience with the versatility, drive, and strength of women. His
outlook was considered controversial by most of his male coun-
terparts. He felt that women should have the right to vote,
form their own organizations, live alone without restrictions,
and enjoy the same employment opportunities as men. He
backed up his convictions by hiring some of the most talented
horsewomen, lady sharpshooters, and actresses in the country
to work in his Wild West show. The popularity of female acts

such as Annie Oakley and Lillian Smith prompted William to add more women riders and ropers to the program. By doing this, he secured his position as a pioneer not only in the entertainment industry but also in the area of women's issues.

The reporter's story, entitled "Colonel Cody Talks," touched on William's views about women and also tried to explain the reason women were inexplicably drawn to him. "Big men [like William Cody] are always gentle to women," the newswoman wrote. "If he isn't a pet with the women he ought to be."[1]

The *New York Recorder* article and those that followed, which were orchestrated by the Wild West show's publicist, Major John Burke, helped generate ticket sales. The country was struggling to make it through a depression, and there was not a lot of money to spend on discretionary items such as entertainment. Consumers could choose between attending Buffalo Bill's Wild West show or Ringling Brothers' program. Women readers who pored over the newspaper reports about the "frontier hero" opted to attend William's show.

In September 1894 William took part in a new form of publicity that promised to increase ticket sales even more. Inventor Thomas Edison made a motion picture featuring Buffalo Bill, Annie Oakley, and a handful of Native Americans from the show. The short recording included demonstrations of their riding and shooting skills and was the forerunner of western movies.[2]

John Burke took full advantage of Edison's finished work and showed the recording at nickelodeons in big cities. John's dedication to promoting Buffalo Bill helped make the showman famous, but it placed an added strain on William's marriage. "Major Burke could think of nothing else but Buffalo Bill," Louisa wrote in her memoirs. "It was blind adoration."[3]

William was besieged by adoring fans everywhere he traveled. His followers included the queen of Belgium; the princesses of Germany, Prussia, and Wales; and Queen Victoria of

England. During his tour of Europe in 1887, Queen Victoria invited the well-known showman and his entourage to perform at the golden jubilee celebration (a golden jubilee marks the fiftieth year of a monarch's reign), and William was honored by the request. The show was held at one of London's largest arenas, Earl's Court Exhibition Grounds. The queen seldom left Buckingham Palace to attend such events; entertainment usually came to her. However, she was so captivated by William and his popularity that she left her home to see the Wild West show. The performance was a huge success. Queen Victoria was impressed with William's troupe of entertainers, in particular the Sioux Indian leader Red Shirt. She thought Red Shirt was one of the most handsome men she had ever seen.[4]

The queen invited William and several cast members of the Wild West show to the palace for tea and spoke of wanting to see the program again. She requested that a command performance be given, and William happily obliged. At the conclusion of the exhibition, she presented William with a signet ring. Newspapers in Europe reported on Queen Victoria and the royal family's enthusiasm for Buffalo Bill and the extravagant gift she had given him. John Burke made sure American papers carried the articles. When Louisa read about the regard that Queen Victoria and Princess Alexandra had for William, she was jealous. She accused the women of paying her "husband improper attention."[5]

According to William, his marriage was on shaky ground when he left for his European tour in late March 1887. He maintained that their relationship suffered because of his wife's irrational jealousy over the women he worked with. Louisa argued that his questionable behavior with female coworkers, show followers, and the like gave her plenty of reason to doubt his faithfulness. They did not correspond with each other at all the first year he was abroad. "I never wrote to her, nor did she write me," William noted in his memoirs.[6]

Louisa did write to Arta, who was overseas with her father. William was thrilled to have his daughter with him. The nineteen-year-old woman doted on him during the European tour, cleaning house for him and running errands. Four-year-old Irma stayed behind with Louisa at the homestead in North Platte. William wrote to his youngest child often.

William constantly worried about the hardships his children had endured because of his troubled marriage. Over the years the girls had overheard several arguments between Louisa and him. On a few occasions when William would leave the house after a particularly loud disagreement, Arta went with him.[7] In 1904 William admitted that she suffered for her faithfulness to him. Louisa often took the anger she had toward her husband out on their children. According to the Codys' divorce records, Louisa would threaten the girls with bodily harm if they ever took their father's side. She warned Irma and Arta that she would pour scalding-hot water on anyone who defied her. "I think she could have been a much better mother in many respects," William told the judge who presided over the divorce hearing. "Although I think she loved her children, she was irritable and cross and peevish with them and many times it was uncalled for."[8]

In February 1905 Mrs. John Boyer, the wife of the former manager of William's North Platte properties, claimed that at times Louisa was cruel to Arta and Irma. Louisa had told the woman that "she had horsewhipped Irma and burned a scar in her face with a lighted match." Mrs. C. P. Davis, a seamstress in the Cody home, admitted to being told about the beatings as well.[9]

Louisa was resentful that William was consistently portrayed in books and magazines as a heroic figure, both on and off the wild plains. She felt that the various indiscretions he enjoyed with some of the women he met should be made public. She reasoned that if his fans and family knew he was a

Outfit worn by Buffalo Bill, and his famous "Lucretia Borgia" gun at the time of the great hunt arranged for the Grand Duke Alexis of Russia (1872)
Buffalo Bill Historical Center, Cody, WY, P.69.126

womanizer, it would have an adverse effect on his image and change his children's inflated opinion of him.

Because the rugged frontier settlements where the Codys lived had no schools, William sent Arta and Irma away to boarding school when they were old enough. However, Louisa didn't allow them to stay at school. As soon as William left home on a hunting or military expedition, she would have the school's staff send them home. "She didn't allow them to remain there as she should have done," William remembered in 1904. "My daughter Irma would have had a much better education if [Louisa] had allowed her to remain."[10]

Louisa's bitterness over William's long absences from home and his involvement with other women affected not only the children but also his friends and sisters, especially Julia and her family. For a while, Louisa managed the North Platte ranch by herself, but when the job became too much, William asked his brother-in-law Al Goodman to take over. Louisa took out her frustrations on Al. He kept William apprised of the difficult situation. "She is a strong woman," William wrote Al in August 1891. "But don't mind her—remember she is my wife—and let it go at that. [If] she gets cranky just laugh at it, she can't help it."[11]

When Al and Julia weren't around, Louisa bad-mouthed William to the Goodmans' son, Ed. Ed wrote letters to his parents about her unkind behavior and the accusation about his being a gossip.

> *I suppose Aunt Lue will do the same by me as she did with brother Will when he was through at North Platte. . . . She will turn the heart of Uncle Will against me if they make up again. As for me saying anything about Aunt Lue that is like a good many more stories; as I never mention their family troubles to anyone . . . until she came and told it herself and everyone knows it by now and they come*

to me to find out particulars but I do not tell them
anything about it at all, but she told everyone.[12]

Many people in William's sphere of influence were aware that he and Louisa were not happily married. They knew that he liked to entertain many guests at the family's ranch in between theatrical seasons and that he had a tendency to drink—at times, too much. According to the court records of their divorce hearing, whenever Louisa objected to William's drinking, he would tell her, "Oh Momma, hush. The only way a man can stand you is to get drunk."[13]

Louisa wanted her husband to herself, but William was too generous with his siblings and their children, as well as noted cast members of the Wild West show, to deny them unlimited access to their home. Frustrated over the lack of private time with her husband and daughters, Louisa was often rude to visitors. William could not understand the reason for Louisa's combative attitude, and the pair quarreled over her actions.[14]

The Codys lived in two different homes when William was in Nebraska. Louisa stayed at their main house in North Platte with the children, and William lived one mile west of the home at Scout's Rest Ranch. Whenever circumstances became unpleasant for him at the main house, he would retreat to the ranch.[15]

When William and Louisa were getting along, they were quite affectionate and loving toward each other. Those times grew less frequent the longer they were married. Louisa repeatedly complained about William's generosity.

If anything should go wrong or that she thought I
wasn't doing the best in a business way, she com-
plained of my giving so much money to different
charitable institutions or for charity. My reply to
that would be, that it was one way that I had of
advertising myself before the public, to let it be
known that I was a charitable man. The public

would appreciate it and when I would go to their towns where they lived to play they would turn out and patronize my entertainment and we would realize more than what I was giving away.[16]

William was more tolerant of Louisa's faults than she was of his. However, he had little patience for one idiosyncrasy: her association with clairvoyants. She regularly consulted fortune-tellers or psychics who prophesied about her future with him. "I tried to tell her that they only done it for money," William remembered in March 1904. "It was trickery and I didn't want her believing it and I positively did not want my children to grow up or made to believe that a fortune teller or anyone else could look into the future and read what their destiny was to be."[17]

Louisa noted in her autobiography that although she and William had their struggles, she could remember being seriously upset with her husband only one time. She believed that she had always done her best to support him in his endeavors, no matter how far apart they might have been. She admitted to sharing his love for the West. "Like my husband, I wanted to be where the smoke did not hang in the atmosphere on gray days," she wrote in her memoirs, "where the sun shone bright and keen and where life was as free as the air."[18]

Bound together by a common desire to conquer the frontier, the Codys endured each other's company, adding to their landholdings and supporting their children in the process. Arta married Horton Boal on June 27, 1889. William was held up in Paris when they wed, and he missed the lavish ceremony. An outbreak of typhoid fever had shut down the city, and no one was allowed to leave.

By the fall of 1890, William was reunited with his sisters (all of whom were married by then), wife, and children. Their time together was brief. "And hardly had he landed," Louisa remarked in her autobiography, "when there came the call for him—the old call of the west, of the saddle and rifle. For the Indians had broken forth in their last campaign on the warpath."[19] Army commander General Nelson Miles asked William to talk with Chief Sitting Bull and try to negotiate the Sioux Indian's surrender. Buffalo Bill and Sitting Bull had become friends in 1885 when the chief toured with the Wild West show for four months. Before William was able to speak with him, though, the Indian leader was shot and killed by members of the Sioux police.

Distressed by Sitting Bull's death and the subsequent events at Wounded Knee, William returned to North Platte and quickly began organizing another trip overseas. Members of his troupe retreated to the Codys' ranch to practice their acts and relax with William before embarking on the next European tour. Louisa was inhospitable and moody, but William encouraged guests to disregard anything hurtful she said or did. Before William left the country, Louisa managed to drive a wedge between Buffalo Bill and his sister Julia. Prodded by her mother, Arta asked her father to give her and her husband the job of taking care of the ranch. Julia and Al were deeply hurt when William terminated their duties and hired his daughter and son-in-law to take their place. The Goodmans moved out of the area to Kansas.[20]

In late 1892 William and more than five hundred cast members sailed home from London after another successful European tour. The following spring Buffalo Bill's Wild West show opened in Chicago. Twenty-five thousand people attended the program daily.[21] Irma and Arta frequently visited their father during the six-month run of the show in the Windy City. Louisa periodically went with them but didn't always let her husband know she was coming. Her surprise visit to William's Chicago hotel room in early 1894 resulted in scandal for the showman. It was then that Louisa discovered the depth of his relationship with actress Katherine Clemmons.

William met Katherine in London and saw great potential in her talent. The porcelain-skinned beauty dreamed of appearing onstage and eagerly accepted William's offer to help finance her career. She traveled with him to Illinois to plan for her theatrical debut in America. The hotel they stayed at in Chicago listed them in the guest registry as man and wife. Louisa was furious when she arrived and learned what was going on. The Codys' marriage survived the affair, and by February 1896 they were adding a new chapter to their tumultuous life together in Wyoming.

William was a key player in the Bighorn Basin project, which included planning and helping to build the town of Cody and digging canals to irrigate the valley and make it prosperous. The *Shoshone Valley Newspaper* ran an article about the Codys and their plans for the territory. William and Louisa were civil to each other during the interview. The reporter saw no evidence that their union had experienced any strain. Not only did he write about how the pair were developing the area, but he also noted how warmly the two treated each other. Those closest to the Codys believed that the article must have been about two other people. As the newspaper story read,

> *It has often been said that Louisa's untiring efforts and unselfish devotion to Colonel Cody has enabled him to reach the highest rounds in the ladder of fame, and indeed we scarcely ever see a popular man where there is not the hand of a devoted wife or mother helping guide him on the road to greatness. Mrs. Cody is a lovely lady in every sense of the word. She is beautiful, too, of the darkest brunette type, and she is intellectual and kind hearted to all.*[22]

Although they were busy with their own lives, Arta and Irma visited their parents in the newly established Wyoming town as often as they could. Irma was finishing her education at a school in Omaha, and Arta was raising her two children, a daughter named Arta Clara and a son named William Cody Boals. Close friends and relatives observed that Louisa and Buffalo Bill's marital problems seemed to fade when they spent time with their grandchildren. They were proud and loving, and nothing else seemed to matter when the grandchildren were around.

With Arta's attention more on taking care of her own family than on running the Nebraska ranch, William approached Julia and Al about returning to their old job. Through letters and several heartfelt conversations, the siblings had been able to repair the damage Louisa and Arta had done to their relationship. "I will give you a 5 to 10 year contract to run that place," William wrote his brother-in-law. "I will agree to any kind of proposition you can suggest to board the help, yourselves, or pay Julia a salary to look after boarding the men. . . . Who works harder than you do? . . . There will be no one to interfere with you anymore than if you owned it."[23]

In October 1896 the entire cast and crew of the Wild West show invaded North Platte to perform at an exhibition William wanted to put on for his hometown. The reception he received at each stop his train made from Omaha, where the show had been stationed, was overwhelming. His sister Helen accompanied him on the journey. "The trip was a continued ovation," she wrote in her memoirs. "Every station was thronged, and Will was obliged to step out on the platform and make a bow to the assembled crowds, his appearance being invariably greeted with a round of cheers. When we reached the station at North Platte, we found that the entire population had turned out to receive their fellow townsman."[24]

Helen eventually transformed the experiences she had with her brother and the tales of his exploits into a book entitled *Last of the Great Scouts*. The tome was her attempt to let his adoring public know how "tender, dedicated and truly

Buffalo Bill's protégée and romantic interest, Katherine Clemmons
The Harvard Theater Collection

kind" her brother was. Published in 1899, the book was an instant best seller. The sales of *Last of the Great Scouts* were enhanced by another tour of the Wild West show across the United States. The show opened in New York in April and abruptly concluded in Kansas City in October when William collapsed after a performance.[25]

A telegram was sent to Louisa informing her that William had typhoid fever. She quickly made arrangements for her husband to be returned to his home in Nebraska. She stayed by his bed watching him drift in and out of sleep. His breathing was short and shallow. Beside him on a nightstand was a hot cup of Garfield tea she had prepared for him. The tea contained twelve drops of a substance known as dragon's blood. Louisa had acquired the concoction from a gypsy who promised that the mixture would act as a love potion. She had served the potion to William twice before, and each time he had become violently ill.[26]

Mrs. John Boyer, one of the Scout's Rest Ranch employees who was aware of the effect the special tea had on Buffalo Bill, witnessed Louisa serving the potion to him a third time. "She will kill him this time sure," she remarked to a coworker. Mrs. Boyer approached Louisa and warned her that if William died, she would report the matter to the authorities and have every doctor examine him. "I will rule him or ruin him," Louisa snapped back.

Rumors that William was not only suffering with typhoid fever but also stricken with a broken heart over his estrangement with his protégée Katherine Clemmons contributed to Louisa's desperate measures. At the Codys' divorce trial, a hired hand swore that he had heard Louisa say, "Before he goes from under my control I'll kill him."[27]

"After taking the Garfield tea Louisa prescribed," William remembered years later, "I became very ill again and said

I didn't care to take any more of these different mixtures." His health slowly improved, but he was afraid to eat or drink anything while staying at the ranch with his wife. "She had threatened to fix me," he testified at his divorce hearing in 1905. "I wasn't going to take a chance of that happening."[28]

SEVEN

The Lady of Venice

———•—•———

*I went down there and they were not looking for me
and I cleaned out the house.*

—LOUISA CODY, TO FRIEND MRS. BOYER IN RESPONSE TO
NEWS THAT WILLIAM HAD A MISTRESS (1905)

On February 17, 1894, the posh Chamberlain Restaurant
in Washington, D.C., was filled to capacity with well-
dressed guests enjoying the elegant ambiance and sumptuous
food. Forty-eight-year-old William Cody was among the fashionably coiffed patrons. Wearing a tailored suit and tie, he was
seated at one of the pristinely set tables. His long hair was
combed neatly away from his handsome face, and his signa-
ture beard and mustache were trimmed and waxed. Katherine
Clemmons, a San Francisco–born actress with soft, stunning
features and a petite frame, sat across from William sipping a
glass of wine and drinking in every word the showman said.
It was obvious from the way he looked at her that the two
were more than just dinner companions. They ate their meal
and shared a bottle of champagne as a handful of musicians
serenaded the patrons with a delicate, classical piece.

In the midst of the harmonious setting, Fred May entered.
Fred, an acquaintance of both William and Katherine, walked
across the eatery to their table. Fred and Katherine exchanged
a flirtatious glance as ordinary pleasantries were exchanged.
Sometime during the tense conversation that transpired
among the three, William punched the man in the face and

knocked him to the floor. The distinguished clientele sitting nearby halted their eating and quietly speculated about what had happened.

The waitstaff hurried to the table and apologized profusely for the disturbance while helping Fred to his feet. With a slight bow and broad grin to the other diners around him, William quickly tried to defuse the awkward situation. "Just a difference of opinion between gentlemen," he told them.[1]

In a few short moments, Fred was gently escorted out of the restaurant, and everything was as it had been before he entered the scene. Katherine took a quick look in the direction Fred had exited, not saying a word. She drank down the wine in front of her and poured herself another glass. William regretted the public incident. He anticipated that the altercation and the woman he was with would make the newspapers. Louisa's suspicions that her husband was involved with Katherine would be confirmed.

Before the meal ended, William decided to return to Wyoming to avoid a potential scandal.

A year before the episode at Chamberlain Restaurant, Louisa had discovered William and Katherine's relationship. In 1893 Mrs. Cody traveled to Chicago, where the Wild West show was on a scheduled stop, to surprise her husband with an impromptu visit. When Louisa arrived in town, she headed straight for William's hotel. She did not give her name when she asked about Buffalo Bill at the reception desk. The clerk informed her that he would be happy to escort her to "Mr. and Mrs. Cody's room." Louisa was furious.[2]

Neither William nor Katherine was in the room when Louisa arrived. The mere thought of her husband betraying her prompted Louisa to charge into the room. She overturned furniture, busted lamps and vases, and knocked items off the walls. When William later met with Louisa, he explained to her that his association with Katherine was strictly professional.

Buffalo Bill escorts the first ladies into the Frost Cave near Cody,
Wyoming (1909)
Buffalo Bill Historical Center, Cody, WY, P.69.846

Louisa accompanied William to Wyoming, while Katherine remained in Washington. Katherine happily entertained the curious press with news of a theatrical production William was financially backing entitled *A Lady in Venice*. She boasted about her dramatic background, her starring role in the play, her relationship with Buffalo Bill, and the $50,000 he had invested in her career.[3]

William met the outspoken, sometimes hard-drinking actress in London in 1887, when the Wild West show was making its first trip through Europe. The nightly show was attended by British kings and queens, Russian dukes, and Austrian princes and princesses. William and his troupe were enthusiastically greeted by royalty and commoners alike. Katherine Clemmons was one of the commoners. He was instantly taken in by her beauty and later referred to her as "the finest looking woman in the world." Fully aware that she had dazzled the showman, Katherine told him about her aspirations for the stage. William thought she was well suited for such a career and offered her an advance of $50,000 to tour the English countryside in a play entitled *Theodore*.

Unfortunately for William, Katherine's acting was not equal to her beauty. Her performances received poor reviews, and ticket sales suffered as a result. The loss of revenue and negative response did not change William's mind about his ingenue. He was confident he could help make her a star.

Viola Katherine Clemmons was born in Palo Alto, California, in 1870. Her father died when she was very young. Katherine, as she preferred to be called, and her sister Ella May were raised by their mother and stepfather. He was employed by the Southern Pacific Railroad as a bookkeeper. Katherine first appeared on the stage of McGuire's San Francisco Opera House in the mid-1880s. Cast in a series of Shakespearean plays, she had the desire but was a less than gifted performer. In an effort to learn more about the craft, she traveled to England to study theater.[4]

William was introduced to Katherine at Earl's Court Exhibition Grounds in London after she had attended one of his shows. The two saw each other often, and when he returned to the United States, Katherine sent him letters through Annie Oakley and Annie's husband, Frank Butler. Katherine gave the Butlers the impression that William had frequently corresponded with her and had sent her numerous telegrams as well. He denied the claim in a letter to Frank written on January 27, 1891. "She is too swift and dishonest for me," William reported. "Those were all lies about her getting letters and cables from me. Would like to know what she done in London and . . . who was the favorite she smiled upon there."[5]

He protested at first, but his impression of Katherine softened after reading her letters. He was too attracted to her uncompromising ambition and drive. His interest in her further heightened after he learned that she was an accomplished horsewoman. Acting as Katherine's agent and manager, William purchased the play *The Lady of Venice* for her. He sent her to the Boston School of Oratory for more theatrical training and made plans for her to open in New York.[6]

The story of *The Lady of Venice* centers around a young woman who disguises herself as a man and subsequently has to fight a duel to defend her honor. Before Katherine's transformation in the play from female to male, she wore an array of exquisite dresses. Critics praised the gowns and the set design but were not as complimentary about her portrayal of the main character. One New York newspaper columnist wrote that Katherine had a "beautiful profile and a lissome figure, but was devoid of acting ability."

William was so enamored with Katherine that he disregarded the press's comments and doubled his efforts to help her. He established a theatrical business for her aptly named The Lady of Venice Company and then hired Sherman Canfield to co-manage the actress's career. Sherman was an exceptional promoter, and William believed he would do a good job for Katherine. Shortly after Sherman accepted the position, William sent him a telegram congratulating him on the decision. Dated September 19, 1893, the telegram read: "Delighted with your work. Whoop her up all week. Wire tonight. Don't spare any money to continue success."[7]

After opening in New York, the show moved on to Boston. However, Katherine continued to get bad reviews, which affected ticket sales. Sherman informed William that the play was suffering financially. William wired more than $6,000 to boost the sinking Lady of Venice Company, but the production continued to lose money. More telegrams were sent to update the showman on the play's decreasing attendance. William wired more funds, but money failed to promote nonexistent talent.

Katherine wasn't as bothered by the criticism of the show and her acting as she was of being separated from William. He was either busy with his own production or on a hunting trip. She conveyed her sentiments in a telegram to William sent in September 1893. The telegram read: "Play roasted. Company roasted. I more than roasted. What will you take for your interest?" William joined Katherine in Boston for the continuation of the play's run, but the material did not fare any better there than it had in New York.[8]

William sent a wire to Sherman, who had gone ahead to make preparations for Katherine's next stop in Chicago. The October 11, 1893, telegram was desperate: "Loss in Boston will be six thousand. Must have explanation and satisfaction or twenty-first finish." Sherman decided to reduce the salaries of the players to cover the cost of the performance in Harrisburg, Pennsylvania, the next stop of the show's run. William instructed the manager to pay off any extraneous cast and crew and then move on without them. "Abandon false ship," his telegram read, "don't want you aboard when storm strikes. You've been too true a friend." William invested another $500 into the play, but it only prolonged the inevitable. By the end of October, he decided to close the run of the production.[9]

After William had facetiously renamed the troupe "The Lady in Ruin Company" and spent more than $80,000 trying to secure a place in the theater for Katherine Clemmons, the play officially reached an end. The curtain rose on the last performance in Washington, D.C., in mid-March 1894. The following month Katherine ended her relationship with William. Disappointed by the close of the play and frustrated by Cody's frequent and long absences away from her, she chose to move on without him. News of their parting was reported in the April 22, 1894, edition of the *Nebraska State Journal*.[10]

*Katherine Clemmons and William F. Cody "Buf-
falo Bill," have parted in both senses of the word.
Miss Clemmons has a very pitiful little tale of woe
about Mr. Cody losing all personal interest in her
and Katherine says she won't have a manager who
does not give personal attention. She says Mr. Cody
shamefully neglected her during her Fifth Avenue
engagement and did nothing whatever for her
beyond paying $40,000 worth of bills. Miss Clem-
mons feels very badly, but she should remember
that Colonel Cody's services have been long and
faithful. . . . He has stood by her and never drawn
his purse string. . . . Colonel Cody has hired first
class companies, leased big theatres, bribed the
critics and lavished annual fortunes upon Miss
Clemmons, yet her failures have been as many as
there were seasons. . . . It is no wonder that even
Colonel Cody's "personal interest" is beginning to
wane. If Miss Clemmons's fancy were for purchas-
ing diamonds or buying up old castles or titles, or
any other inexpensive fads, Mr. Cody would gladly
gratify her, but the stage is all together too expensive as an amusement.*[11]

William was sad when his affiliation with Katherine
ended. Public discussion about their affair was far from over,
however. Branded a "wearisome actress" and a "money driven
opportunist" by theatrical critics and disappointed Buffalo Bill
Cody fans, Katherine sought the attention of multimillionaire
Howard Gould. Howard was a yachtsman, an auto racer, and a
globe-trotting chum of European royalty, who had a weakness
for actresses. The fledgling starlet and the son of a prosperous
New York financier were married on October 12, 1898. For
more than nine years, Howard lavished expensive jewels and
clothing on Katherine. He also purchased thousands of acres

of undeveloped land in Sand Point, New York, to build a new home for her.[12]

For a while the Manhattan society pages praised Gould and Clemmons's union. Katherine's background was reinvented to make for better reading. Where she was born, the professional training she received in the arts, and the famous followers who supposedly bolstered her career were all a fabrication. The reporters also claimed that the couple was "ecstatically happy." That too was a falsehood. The marriage became rocky shortly after they wed. Katherine sued Howard for a divorce on May 13, 1907. The details of their sordid troubles were revealed in the *Covington Sun Newspaper* on April 16, 1908.[13]

That portion of the public which has been waiting so patiently for the oft-delayed washing of the family linen of the Howard Goulds is about to have its reward. Before Justice Dowling Mrs. Gould's attorney, Clarence J. Shearn, made a motion to have the issues framed for trial by jury on the ground that they were of such a nature that no judge could care to pass on them first.

Sounding a note of self-pity as he surveyed the miserably unhappy life he had led since he had married Katherine Clemmons, Howard Gould told of the many humiliations to which he had been subjected.

There are allegations of the deepest import to the wife of the millionaire, however, in the answer. Gould charged that not only before but after he married Katherine Clemmons she was guilty of improper conduct with Colonel William F. Cody.

There are charges of Mrs. Gould's fondness for intoxicants, beginning, as alleged, with two or three cocktails before breakfast, a pint of Hock at luncheon, brandy highballs and unlimited supplies of

champagne at dinner, whereby on one occasion, it is
alleged she fell from her chair to the floor.

Mr. Gould alleges that his marriage was the
result of fraud and misrepresentation on the part of
his wife. He says that Mrs. Gould, prior to the mar-
riage, asserted that her relations with Colonel Cody
were exclusively of a business nature, whereas they
were meretricious. He swears that during 1887,
1889 and 1892 his present wife lived with Cody in
London, Paris, Chicago, Nebraska, Virginia and
New York.[14]

News of Katherine and William's affair was made public during the Codys' divorce case in 1905. The Goulds' long,
drawn-out divorce case kept Katherine and William's names
in newspapers across the country for close to two years. The
image of the heroic buffalo hunter and family man was tar-
nished in many followers' eyes.

The Goulds' divorce was finalized in early 1909. Howard
was ordered to pay Katherine $36,000 a year in alimony, the
largest sum a court had ever ordered to be paid. She responded
to the settlement by saying, "It's hard to dress well on less
than $40,000 a year in Manhattan."[15]

On November 4, 1910, Katherine again made the news
while residing in Lynchburg, Virginia; the divorcee claimed
that someone was trying to kill her. According to an article in
the *New York Times*, Katherine reported that three attempts
had been made on her life.

Mrs. Katherine Clemmons Gould, former wife of
Howard Gould, came here [Lynchberg Hospital]
last night from her country home, Blue Gap Farm,
to receive medical attention for what she thought
was poisoning. The physician found no need to
treat Mrs. Gould and no evidence of poisoning. The
former Mrs. Gould drove here during the night

> *behind a team of mules which she lashed all the ten*
> *miles of the journey. Greatly excited, she summoned*
> *a physician and said she had eaten "queer-tasting*
> *food." She raved wildly. The physician, after exami-*
> *nation, said she had taken no poison and that her*
> *trouble was merely extreme nervousness.*[16]

Katherine Clemmons died on October 13, 1930, in Lynch-burg, Virginia. She was sixty-seven years old. She left $11,000 in cash to her sister Ella May as well as $80,000 in real estate.

EIGHT

The Cody Trials

―――•――

She drove away my friends. When they were no longer
welcome, it was no longer my home.

—WILLIAM CODY, IN REMARKS TO THE COURT DURING HIS
DIVORCE PROCEEDINGS (FEBRUARY 29, 1905)

Water sloshed out of buckets being passed quickly between
the people standing in front of a house fire in the little town of North Platte, Nebraska. The water was frantically
tossed onto the flames rising from William and Louisa Cody's
ornate, three-story home in the winter of 1890. With the help
of friends and neighbors, the small volunteer fire brigade managed to hold off the blaze long enough for Louisa and daughter
Irma to rescue several possessions from the home. The inferno
eventually overtook the house the Codys called Welcome Wigwam. Many valuable souvenirs and mementos from Wild West
shows performed around the world were lost in the fire.

William was on a trip to the north plains to meet with
Sitting Bull when he was notified by telegram that the house
was about to burn down. According to his sister Helen, "His
response was characteristically Buffalo Bill."

"Save Rosa Bonheur's painting," he wrote, "and the house
may go to blazes."[1] Although Louisa would have preferred her
husband's initial concerns to have been about her and the
children, she wasn't surprised by his reply. She told a friend
that William held an attachment for anything presented to
him from women who gave him enormous attention.

Rosa Bonheur's painting was among Buffalo Bill's most prized possessions. In 1889 the famous seventy-year-old artist and sculptor painted a portrait of William on his favorite horse, Tucker. It showed the strong, proud showman leading his majestic ride around a grove of trees. Rosa's work hung in the parlor beside a painting of the Codys' son, Kit. The brilliant image was featured on the Wild West show's playbills, postcards, and posters. The public so admired the painting that art collectors across the United States sought out Rosa to paint more scenes of the American West.[2]

Rosa was twenty-four years older than William when she painted his portrait, but the vast age difference did not keep Louisa from feeling threatened. She was aware of the hours that went into producing such a work of art and was jealous of any woman able to spend long periods of time with her husband.

Within a year of the Codys' home burning, William rebuilt Welcome Wigwam. Louisa lived in the town house for more than sixteen years. She decorated it with lace curtains, gigantic mountain-scene paintings, saddles, and Indian relics. William occasionally stayed with her at the home when he was in the area, but he spent the bulk of his Nebraska visits at Scout's Rest Ranch. His practice of inviting many guests to stay for long periods of time at their house always annoyed Louisa. Her public outbursts over the revolving door of company embarrassed him. He reasoned that they could avoid such scenes if they lived in separate homes.

Louisa was not opposed to every guest who visited the Cody home. She graciously welcomed local businessmen and potential Wild West show investors who came for dinner. She oversaw the meal preparations, conducted tours of the property, and helped William present gifts to their callers in appreciation for their support.[3]

Louisa was an impeccable hostess at their daughter Irma's wedding on February 24, 1903. The grand military ceremony between the Codys' youngest child and cavalry officer Lieutenant Clarence Armstrong Stott was lavishly decorated with yellow flowers and yellow ribbons. William was traveling through England with the Wild West show and could not attend the nuptials. In addition to his usual duties with the program, William had to do the job his business partner, Nate Salsbury, usually did. Nate had passed away on December 24, 1902, from stomach trouble.[4] Louisa tried to make up for William's absence by giving Irma a gigantic cake, a lace gown, expensive jewelry, and an assortment of other wedding gifts.[5]

William shared his disappointment in not attending his daughter's wedding with his sister Julia. In a letter dated December 29, 1902, he explained his frustration. "Mr. Salsbury's death gives me more work," William wrote. "I won't be able to come over to Irma's wedding, or attend to business, or to get a day's rest."[6]

The frequency of William's letters to Julia increased after her husband died in 1901. He often wrote her about his feelings for Louisa and their rocky marriage. Ironically, while Louisa was helping plan Irma's wedding, William was seeking Julia's counsel about a divorce. He wrote her in March 1902:

> *Julia, I have tried and tried to think that it was right for me to go on through all my life, living a false lie. Just because I was too much of a morral* [sic] *coward to do otherwise. But I have decided that if the law of man can legally join together the same law can legally unjoin. . . . There's no use of my telling you of my married life—more than that it grows more unbearable each year—Divorces are not looked down upon now as they used to be—people are getting more enlightened. . . . God did not intend joining two persons together for both to go through life miserable. When such a mistake was made—a law was created to undo the mistake. As it is I have*

Mrs. William F. Cody—"Lulu"
Buffalo Bill Historical Center, Cody, WY, P.69.203

*no future to look forward to—no happiness or even
contentment. Lulu will be better contented. She will
be her absolute master—I will give her every bit of
the North Platte property. And an annual income.
If she will give me a quiet legal seporation [sic]—if
she won't do this then it's war and publicity. I hope
for all concerned it may be done quickly. Wish you
could have a talk with Arta.*[7]

Thirty-seven-year-old Arta held a grudge against her
father for a variety of reasons, not the least of which was his
disloyalty to her mother and how his unfaithfulness made
Louisa feel. William had not attended Arta's first wedding,
and the long periods of time he spent away from the family
had created a distance between father and daughter. She was
aware that he was contemplating divorce, and she strongly
objected to the idea. In December 1902 William embarked
on a four-year tour of Europe, and the two could not discuss
the matter face-to-face. Arta was close to her aunt Julia, and
together they ran the daily business at the Irma Hotel in
Cody, Wyoming. William prevailed upon Julia to speak to Arta
for him and explain his position. Julia agreed.

Rather than trying to be understanding, Arta became
more angry that her father would even consider leaving her
mother. In her estimation the situation wasn't that serious.
She sided with Louisa in thinking that he only wanted a
divorce so that he could marry another woman.[8] Arta wrote
a letter to her father listing Louisa's good points and asking him to reconsider getting a divorce. He respected Arta
for championing her mother, but remained firm in his decision to end the marriage. "Well, it's war now," he wrote his
sister in July 1903. "I got the first cross letter today that Arta
ever wrote me. But I am going through with it [the divorce].
I think I'm entitled to be at peace in my old age. And I surely
can't have it with Lulu."[9]

In hope of reconciling with Arta, William returned to the United States around Christmas in 1903. Arta was to be married to Dr. Charles Thorp on New Year's Day 1904. Her first husband had died five years prior, and she was excited about a second chance at love. The small affair was held in Denver. Tensions ran high between Louisa and William, but they survived the day without a squabble. Not long after the ceremony, William returned to London, where the Wild West show was scheduled to perform.[10]

Less than a month after Arta had remarried and moved to Spokane, Washington, with her new husband, she passed away. Complications that arose from an operation to correct "organic trouble" claimed her life. Louisa claimed she died of a broken heart caused by her father's behavior. Given the sad circumstance, William suggested that he and Louisa set aside their differences and focus on their daughter's burial.[11] Grief-stricken and bitter, she lashed out at William for ever discussing their personal relationship with Arta. According to his sister May, Louisa wanted to charge him with murder. She attributed Arta's "organic trouble" to her being upset over William's talk of divorce. May managed to change Louisa's mind about publicly making such an outrageous claim. Instead, Louisa chose to send William a telegram accusing him of breaking their child's heart.[12]

The Codys accompanied Arta's body to Rochester, New York, where she was to be laid to rest beside her brother and sister. For the bulk of the journey, William and Louisa did not speak to each other. William tried to engage Louisa in conversation and invited her to ride in the coach with him to their child's gravesite, but she wanted nothing to do with him. Her anger over the death of their daughter and what seemed to be the end of her marriage eventually got the better of her, and when they were changing trains in Chicago, she made a scene. "It's your fault," she screamed venomously at William. "I will bring you Codys down so low the dogs won't bark at you," she tearfully vowed.[13]

By June 13, 1904, William had had enough, and he legally filed for divorce. The suit, filed at the Big Horn County District Court, claimed that Louisa was a "nag" and that she and William were "incompatible." It also noted that she had threatened his life numerous times. Louisa countersued, citing William's infidelity as the reason for their marital difficulties.[14]

The divorce trial was delayed a number of times not only because Louisa contested the action but also to give her a chance to care for her ailing father. Once John Frederici's condition stabilized, the hearing was set to begin at 10:00 a.m. on February 16, 1905.

Newspapers everywhere predicted that a "tidal wave of shocking accusations and deeply personal information would flood the courtroom during the trial and leave the spectators in attendance, drowning in a sea of disillusionment." William was upset that the case would be front-page news. "I was afraid and feared that it would, as I am a public man," he told the judge presiding over the hearing. "But I took every step and every means in my power to keep this family trouble out of the public press."[15]

The transcription of the Codys' bitter divorce case was uncovered at a college library in Casper, Wyoming, in November 1979 and was then made public by the State Archives Department in Cheyenne. (The county clerk at the time speculated that the "information may have been secreted by design to prohibit access to out of court testimonies.")[16]

The aged records showed that the wife of the foreman of the Codys' ranch property was the first witness to be heard at the trial. Mrs. John Boyer testified about Louisa's behavior at home. She informed the court that "Mrs. Cody had an argumentative disposition and that her rampages made life at home very difficult for Buffalo Bill, their children, and any guests who visited." Mrs. Boyer also confirmed William's claim that Louisa had tried to poison him, citing that on three separate occasions she saw Louisa put drops of dragon's blood into her husband's coffee and tea. When Mrs. Boyer was asked if Louisa had told her why she had given him the drug, she replied, "Mrs. Cody believed the dragon's blood would make her husband love her." William's penchant for drinking was made known to the court by the same witness. Louisa was able to slip the drug easily to him once he was inebriated.[17]

William's attorneys called Mrs. H. S. Parker to the stand next. Mrs. Parker testified that Louisa had told her she had poisoned the prized staghounds given to William by the tsar of Russia and that she had done it "just for spite." William tried to save the animals with a remedy of hot grease and mustard but was unsuccessful. He initially accused the ranch foreman of giving them lethal doses of strychnine. The foreman denied any involvement and informed William that Louisa was the one who had killed the dogs. Stunned by the news, Cody confronted his wife. "I told her how inhumane it was for her to poison my beautiful dogs," he said to the court. "At this she became very angry and walked away."[18]

Louisa's cruelty to Irma was also brought up in the trial. In addition, Mrs. Parker testified that Mrs. Cody had consulted fortune-tellers. "She said she paid a fortune teller in Battle Creek, Michigan $35.00 for her services," Mrs. Parker told the court. "The Battle Creek prophet told her that the Colonel had lived five years too long."[19]

A third witness close to the Codys swore that Louisa had told her about William's infidelities. Louisa described her husband to Mrs. C. P. Davis as a drunkard who "had dallied with other women throughout their entire marriage."

Louisa's attorneys put a number of people on the stand who confirmed her claim. Some told the court that "Louisa was a lonely woman with a legitimate right to be upset with

William." Family friend Joseph Iddings stated that Buffalo Bill never took Louisa with him on any of his trips after they settled in North Platte. William denied the statement and accused Joseph of lying. "No one knows it better than himself," William insisted in court, "for he personally knows that Mrs. Cody has traveled with me at many times when I have been traveling throughout the United States giving exhibitions. I will further state that Mrs. Cody has visited with me in nearly every large city in the United States and I doubt if there is a lady in the land outside of the profession of an actress or a showman, that have visited so many cities as Mrs. Cody has."[20]

In defending himself against the assertion that he was a drunkard, William stated that Louisa never complained to him much about his drinking. "She said that I was always better natured and more liberal and pleasanter around the house when I was drinking than when I was not."[21]

When attorneys questioned William about his extramarital affairs, he was contrite and a bit embarrassed. Among the names of the various women he was accused of being involved with were actress Katherine Clemmons and press agent Bessie Isbell, who was named as co-respondent in the Codys' divorce case. Louis Clark, one of the foremen at William's TE Ranch on the South Fork of the Shoshone, who witnessed William and Bessie together in Wyoming, testified that there was "undue intimacy" between the two. Other witnesses who took the stand during the trial claimed that William was involved with "four or five nice Indian girls . . . and other women on different occasions and at different times in his life."[22]

According to the February 28, 1905, edition of the *Denver Post,* Louisa was quiet and somewhat dazed by the proceedings. When it was her turn to testify, she "walked with a firm step to the stand and took the oath. She did not appear to be nervous or hesitant."

"Mrs. Cody did not look much different from other women of advanced years who are beginning to show the effects of age and many cares," the article continued. "Her hair is tinged with gray, and her fair features show some of the wrinkles of time, but her eyes were bright and her thin lips were pressed close together. Clasping her hands in her lap, Mrs. Cody prepared for the trying ordeal through which she passed and has dreaded, but the result of which she did not appear to fear."[23]

Louisa spoke calmly about her thirty-four years of marriage to William. She fondly described their courtship, engagement, and wedding. Of their time at Fort McPherson, she recalled that they were financially strapped. William's pay as a scout barely made ends meet, and Louisa supplemented their income with sewing projects. Things improved monetarily when William's Wild West show was launched. William was disgusted by Louisa's claim that he couldn't afford to take care of his young family. He denied the statement over and over again.

Buffalo Bill's lawyers asked Louisa a series of questions about her life with the famous showman. They grilled her about witnesses' statements claiming that she was rude to the people who visited William at their home and had cursed guests who wouldn't leave them alone. She denied ever behaving in such a manner. The attorneys took extra time to go over the accusation that she had poisoned William. "I don't know what dragon's blood is," she told the judge. "I never saw any and never heard of such a thing. I did doctor my husband and give him medicine for his troubles when he drank."[24]

With reference to poisoning his dogs, she insisted that she didn't do it intentionally. The strychnine was set out to kill rats that had been seen in the barns. Louisa professed to feel as heartbroken about the dogs' deaths as William did.

Lawyers concluded their examination of Louisa with a question that stunned the courtroom. "Do you still love Mr.

Cody?" the attorney inquired. "Yes," she replied. "He's the father of my children and I love him still." A follow-up question was asked about whether she wanted a reconciliation. "Yes, I do," she quickly responded. "I would gladly welcome him home."[25]

For many major newspapers, William's time on the stand during the hearing was front-page material. Everything from his manner of dress to the number of female Buffalo Bill Cody fans who attended the trial was reported on. William's friends advised him against taking the stand in his own defense. They feared that an attack from Louisa's attorney would cause irreparable harm to his reputation. William believed that his testimony would strengthen his case, and by showing he wasn't afraid to face the enemy, he could win favor for his cause.

Louisa's lawyers were tough on William. In addition to having the showman restate specific instances that prompted family, friends, and business associates to leave the Codys' Nebraska homes when they visited, they also pressed him to give the names of all those people. "Louisa's unbearable conduct at all times was the culprit," William told the court. "There were so many of them (family, friends, etc.) that I could not recall the names."

"Can you name a single person that by reason of Mrs. Cody's actions was compelled to leave your home?" the lawyer asked again.

"There were several of them, but I don't care to mention their names because they will be present at the trial to answer the question," William replied.

"Do you refuse, Colonel, at this time, to give the name of a single person?" the lawyers persisted.

Again William refused to offer any names. "Newspapers have in some way got a hold of what this testimony is that I am now giving and I do not, will not, give out any names," he snapped. "These friends of mine who are to be witnesses would not like to have their names mentioned at present. I do not want this case tried in the newspapers, but I propose to have this case tried in court."[26]

Early in his testimony William stated that there had always been problems between him and Louisa, almost from the moment they were married. He implied that his feelings for his wife had lessened after so many years of hearing her complain, but Louisa's attorney challenged that notion by having him read aloud several letters William had written to her. The affectionate letters, dated as late as 1900, noted how proud he was of Louisa and how much she meant to him.[27]

When the courtroom questions eventually surfaced about William's relationship with Katherine Clemmons, an uncomfortable hush fell over the gallery area. His response was short. He denied having intimate relations with the actress at any time. He was also asked if he had had improper relations with members of England's royal family. His attorneys objected to the names of innocent parties being "dragged into the case."

On redirect, William was given the chance to defend himself against the claims that he was insensitive and a habitual philanderer. He told the court how he felt he treated his wife. "I was universally kind to her," he insisted, "and I defy any man or woman to swear that they ever heard me speak an unkind or cross word to her. . . . I am liberal with everyone and especially with my family and always have been. And I have always been in a position to give my wife and my family more money than most men have. And I always look to the comfort and support of my family first above all things."[28]

Toward the end of the hearing, it was revealed that William had at one time or another offered to pay off Louisa's debts and the mortgage on their property in North Platte if she would agree to a quiet, uncontested divorce. A telegraph sent to her on August 21, 1900, stood as proof of the offer. William wrote: "Ranch is yours. Take it and run it to suit yourself." Louisa's lawyers sought clarification on the claim. According to Mrs. Cody, William offered to deed her the property at North Platte, including Scout's Rest Ranch, because he wanted her to keep it for their old age. "I deeded to Mrs. Cody the residences and the town property and part of the Scout's Rest Ranch," William explained, "so as to have less nagging and a little peace." Later in his testimony he added that "Louisa refused to grant my request for a peaceful settlement and furthermore stated that she was going to fight a divorce to the bitter end. But with all those threats, I am willing to forget and forgive them, providing she will give me a legal separation."[29]

Nothing would entice Louisa to go along with a divorce. She made it clear to the courts that she would not let William go. When asked by the reporter outside the courthouse why she wanted to stay bound to William, she reiterated her love for him because he was the father of her children. She told them that "Will was the kindest and most generous of men."[30]

The Codys' divorce attorneys delivered their final summations almost a month after the case was initially filed. Before rendering his decision, the judge ordered that the names of the women who were listed as being romantically involved with William be stricken from the record. The judge believed that he had not been provided with enough evidence to support the claim that William was having an affair with any of them, and therefore that it would be unjust for them to be linked to the legal proceedings.

The judge further ruled that the charges leveled by both William and Louisa were baseless. He did not believe that Louisa had tried to poison William; instead, he felt that she had merely tried to cure his hangover. He stated that her motives had been misunderstood and that William was guilty of drinking to excess. The judge was inclined to believe that Louisa was proud of her husband's achievements and wanted to work out their problems.[31]

On March 23, 1905, the judge in the trial *Cody v. Cody*
denied William's petition for divorce. His lawyers appealed
and two months later stood before another judge in Cheyenne. The petition was denied there too, but William remained
hopeful. He told the press that he would take his request to
the Supreme Court. He left his attorney with the job of filing
the proper documents and headed to France for a five-month
engagement with the Wild West show.[32]

While William was overseas, he bombarded Julia with letters about how his life had changed. His finances had taken a
hit as a result of the trial and the bad publicity that came with
it. He wanted to reassure his sister that he would recover and
regain what had been lost. He wrote on June 14, 1905:

> *No thanks, Sister for the money to make the payment*
> *on the house. I only wish that some day I will be*
> *able to do much more for you. And all my sisters who*
> *have been good and true to me. . . . And it's in my old*
> *age I have found God. . . . And realize how easy it*
> *is to abandon sin and serve him. When one stops to*
> *think how little they have to give up to serve God. . . .*
> *It's a wonder so many more don't do it. A person only*
> *has to do right, through his knowledge. I have quit*
> *drinking entirely. . . . I am doing a nice business. And*
> *everything is running smooth. And I hope to make*
> *a lot of money before coming home. . . . I must fix*
> *myself for my old age—and for those I love.*[33]

Among the letters William received from Julia and the
others he loved was one from his daughter Irma. In it, the
twenty-two-year-old woman made a heartfelt request that he
withdraw his petition for divorce. William carefully considered the earnest plea from his only living child and promised
Irma that he would stay married to Louisa forever.[34]

NINE

A Wandering Heart

———◆———

I still love my husband just as I always did. We were always happy until he went into show business, and met other people—other women. I always hoped he would settle down with me some day at our home in North Platte.

—LOUISA CODY (1905)

The lobby of the elegant, multistory hotel in downtown Sherman, Texas, was busy with fashionably dressed guests in various stages of checking in and out of the establishment. Attentive staff members, their arms bulging with luggage, escorted guests to their rooms or to the exit of the building. John Claire, William Cody's valet, weaved through the preoccupied patrons as he made his way to the front desk. En route to the counter, he passed a giant sandwich-board sign covered with an image of Buffalo Bill on his horse. Several excited children huddled around the poster and chatted happily about the famous scout's upcoming performance.

An overly eager clerk enthusiastically greeted John as he walked to the front desk. They exchanged pleasantries, and after the clerk handed John a stack of William's mail, he sheepishly asked if John could get Cody's autograph for him. "It's not for me," he insisted. "It's for my son." John nodded and then continued with his duties. Before going upstairs, he retrieved one of William's costumes from the laundry along with a bottle of exhalia, a medicinal substance used to soothe aching muscles.

Once John finished the first of the day's many tasks, he proceeded to the grand staircase leading to the stylish, oversized suites. He gave a couple of knocks on William's door and routinely entered the room before an invitation was given. William was lying in bed, and Miss Bessie Isbell was seated beside him. John was taken aback to see her there, but the appealing twenty-three-year-old woman was unmoved. According to the valet's recollections years after the uncomfortable scene, Bessie was dressed provocatively. "She was draped in a garment that consisted of two pieces," John announced at the Codys' divorce trial, "namely, a loose waist, a sort of Kimono ladies generally wear I understand in their private boudoir. The other piece of wearing apparel consisted of an underskirt. She didn't seem inclined to leave until Colonel Cody requested her to do so."

The valet watched Bessie draw her loose gown close to her and then lean down and kiss William on the cheek. "Until later, my Pahaska," John remembered her saying.[1] (Pahaska was the Indian name given to Buffalo Bill. It means "Long Hair.")

John was employed with the Wild West show from 1899 to 1902. He acted as the show's booking agent and advertising representative, among other jobs. During the theatrical season of 1900, John was William's personal valet. He retrieved Cody's mail, looked after Cody's clothes, was his personal dresser for each performance, made sure that Cody's sleeping accommodations were acceptable, and was available for whatever the showman might require at any time. "I was always in close contact with him," John testified at the Codys' divorce trial.

Whereas most people could only speculate about William's extramarital affairs, John swore he could attest to at least one of the women Buffalo Bill was rumored to be seeing. Bessie

Isbell was not the first woman William was linked to romantically. However, she would be the last mistress Mrs. Cody would tolerate. Bitter over the betrayal and fed up with her husband's philandering, Louisa listed Bessie as co-respondent in the divorce suit William filed.[2]

During the 1905 divorce trial, some of the soldiers William served with at Fort McPherson, Nebraska, testified that his penchant for other women dated as far back as 1869, less than four years after he and Louisa were married. M. Blake of the Fifth Cavalry noted that William was "always surrounded by a bevy of dusky maidens employed at a house of ill fame in Cottonwood Canyon." Blake told the court that William spent the bulk of his time there with a young woman named Vicky Howard. "She often told me herself that he paid her room and board for 16 or 17 weeks," the soldier stated to the court. He noted that William frequented other such businesses and kept other women. "He visited Dave Perry's house at North Platte, run by a woman by the name of Lizz or Lizzie," the soldier added. He went on to say that William was "one of the business's most popular guests."

"No matter where I went with him there were always other women," Blake continued with a hint of animosity toward the famous showman. "Cody was made a little God of in that post [Fort McPherson], the officers surrounded him, boozed him up pretty well, and got up all sorts of games there and sports in honor of Buffalo Bill. . . . The Poncho Indian Reservation was quiet across the river, and we all had skiffs and canoes in the evening to go across to the reservation to have a good time with the Indian maidens. Bill had his share of them as well as the rest of us. He had three or four pretty ones that he picked out for his own use."[3]

Bessie Isbell was one of many women who sought William's attention in the late 1800s and early 1900s. Little is known of the early life of the beauty Buffalo Bill insisted was his publicity agent. She was born in 1872 in Virginia. Her parents were highly educated people, as were their parents before them. Trained in the field of law, both of her grand-fathers were judges. Bessie and her sister were living off an inheritance from their grandfather when she decided to work with the Wild West show. Her duties were to advertise and sell Helen Cody Wetmore's book about Buffalo Bill entitled *Last of the Great Scouts*. Bessie often worked in advance of the show, handing out flyers and posting advertisements about the program and Wetmore's popular biography.[4]

During the time Bessie toured with the Wild West show, which most historical accounts list as the 1900 theatrical season, William was traveling to the performances in his new private railroad coach. In addition to the changes in his mode of transportation and his traveling companion, the show also underwent a transformation. His cast was no longer acting out Custer's Last Stand but was now reenacting the Battle of San Juan Hill. Wherever the show appeared throughout the East and the Midwest, fans enthusiastically cheered the program and its star. Fifty-four-year-old William was encouraged by the overwhelming reception to the alterations in the production.[5]

The show was doing well, but William was concerned about the overwhelming cost of maintaining the enormous event and his other business ventures. Some of the funds from the program were being used for the continual development of Cody, Wyoming; an irrigation project in the Bighorn Basin; and gold and copper mining operations in Arizona. Bessie was a pleasant distraction from the monetary struggles. Although William maintained that she was a good press agent and a necessary addition to the staff of advance publicists, not everyone connected with the program believed she was on the Wild West show's payroll.[6]

In his deposition given during the Codys' divorce trial,

William F. Cody dressed for winter in a buffalo coat,
circa 1915
Buffalo Bill Historical Center, Cody, WY, P.69.318

John Claire insisted that Bessie was not an employee of William's show. He stated that she was simply Buffalo Bill's mistress. William denied the allegation and claimed that they were simply good friends. He told the court that Bessie's salary was $25 a week plus expenses. John testified that William specifically told him the two were lovers. He swore that William gave Bessie money and expensive presents; John also stated that he packed some of those gifts in Cody's private car when the William and Bessie traveled together. One of the presents was a stride saddle engraved with both of their names. (According to several historians, William gave saddles to a variety of women over the course of his career. He considered it a pleasure to present them with gifts as a token of his appreciation for their work with the Wild West show. Among the many recipients were Lulu Parr, Mrs. Johnnie Baker, and Annie Oakley.)

William and Bessie were seen together numerous times in hotel rooms in different cities where the Wild West show was scheduled to play. "The couple were inseparable," John recalled in court. "Bessie visited Cody in his tent before and after performances in Philadelphia, Minneapolis, Chicago, and New Orleans. . . . I saw her place her hands on Cody's shoulders as they left his tent one evening. She pinned a rose on the Colonel's coat and said: 'Here's a rose for you, Colonel.'"[7]

William was insulted by the accusation that there was anything inappropriate about his relationship with Bessie. "Ms. Isbell was one of my agents," he argued in his deposition in 1905. "Most of my agents called on me during the time I was busy in my hotel room or tent, and they came for instructions."[8] Eyewitness accounts of the pair kissing, holding hands, and riding alone in the carriage used to transport William back and forth to the show grounds made Louisa doubt that Bessie was simply a business associate. She hired a private detective to investigate her husband and Bessie. The detective reported that "Buffalo Bill and Ms. Isbell have been on too friendly of terms for some time." John agreed with the detective's findings and went on to tell the court about the affectionate letters and telegrams Bessie and William sent to each other whenever they were apart. Louisa's attorneys questioned William about the correspondences, and he did not deny they communicated. He maintained, however, that he was only being kind and supportive. Bessie had contracted tuberculosis, and he only wanted to help her through the illness.

The extent of William's benevolence toward Bessie was the source of heated debate during the divorce hearing. Louisa's lawyers grilled Buffalo Bill about the support he gave Bessie. When pressed, he admitted to "having bought a ranch and transferring the ownership to her for $1 and other considerations." When asked what those "other considerations" were, William said he "didn't remember."[9]

Another woman William was romantically linked to was the author Olive Logan Sikes. Reference was made to her during the Codys' divorce hearing. Olive wrote for the House of Beadle and Adams, a publishing firm responsible for several dime novels about Buffalo Bill and his daring exploits. Olive was an actress and lecturer as well as a novelist. Born in April 1839 in Elmira, New York, she made her stage debut at the age of five. After attending Wesleyan Female Seminary, she became a playwright and a contributor to numerous periodicals, including *Beadle and Adams Dime and Nickel Handbooks.*

A chance introduction to William Cody at the New York publishing company in 1885 sparked rumors that the accomplished writer would be penning a new novel about Buffalo Bill's adventures. There was no truth to the talk, as William's novels were written either by himself or by Prentiss Ingram. When the rumors about Olive reached Louisa, she was quick to believe them and was jealous. William assured his wife that what she heard was just gossip, but she remained suspicious of Olive and extremely jealous that the author's and her husband's names were linked.[10]

In 1871 Olive married Wirt Sikes, a fellow novelist with the house of Beadle and Adams. The couple moved to London, where Wirt died in 1883. Olive became demented and was committed to an asylum in Banstead, England. She died on April 27, 1909.[11]

Friends and acquaintances of both William and Louisa claimed that William "had an appetite for any beautiful woman he met; it didn't make any difference, there was no exception."[12] Advocates and admirers of the showman suggest that his natural inclination to help anyone in need, combined with his flirtatious manner, was often misconstrued. Such was the case with his association with Nadeau Piatt, a young woman with unspecified ties to William's mining venture in Pima County, Arizona. On occasion the pair wrote each other to share information about the project. Her letters to him began "Dear B.B." (for "Buffalo Bill"). His letters to her began the same way, but in his case "B.B." meant "Beautiful Baby." The tone of the greeting prompted some of William's friends to think that the pair were more than business colleagues, but the letters seemed to be the extent of their relationship.[13]

The conclusion of the 1900 theater season was marred with tragedy for Buffalo Bill. His brother-in-law Al Goodman, who had been like a father to him, passed away, and a major train accident near Louisville, Kentucky, claimed the lives of several of the Wild West show's horses, destroyed William's private car, and nearly crippled Annie Oakley. The life-changing events left Cody with little time or interest in Bessie or any other woman outside of his immediate family.

His daughters joined him in New York in August 1901, two months after the train wreck. The Wild West show was to perform at Madison Square Garden, and William wanted his children around him when he wasn't hosting the nightly extravaganza. According to John Claire, Bessie left for Wyoming just before Irma and Arta arrived. Believing the climate would be good for Bessie's health, William suggested that she stay at his ranch in the Bighorn country.

After more than three years with the Wild West show, Bessie and William parted company. Her tuberculosis was advancing, and she decided to travel to the desert country of the Holy Land to live out the remainder of her days.[14]

Ten

The Sharpshooter

———————•———————

*To the loveliest and truest little woman both in heart
and aim, in all the world.*

—WILLIAM F. CODY, IN A NOTE TO ANNIE OAKLEY (1890)

In April 1885 the sun-bleached wooden grandstand in
Louisville, Kentucky, which ordinarily surrounded a well-
maintained baseball field, overlooked Buffalo Bill Cody's Wild
West set. The plush, green outfield was filled with scenes
depicting the wild frontier, and the infield had been transformed into a parade ground for horses, buffalo, and steers. A
number of members of the show's cast stood in a line in front
of home plate patiently waiting to be introduced to a petite,
unassuming young woman named Annie Oakley. William and
the manager of the Wild West show, Nate Salsbury, had signed
a contract with the expert riflewoman to appear in the historical program, and they were anxious for her to meet the rest
of the cast.[1]

Cowboys, Indian warriors and chiefs, and vaqueros greeted
the pretty woman with a hearty handshake and a warm welcome. "There I was facing the real Wild West," Annie recalled
in her memoirs, "the first white woman to travel with what
society might have considered an impossible outfit."[2] Buffalo
Bill affectionately referred to Annie as Missie and positioned
the talented markswoman at the start of his show. According to William's sister Julia, Annie's act "always brought the
crowds to their feet."[3]

Annie Oakley and Frank Butler, her husband and manager, traveled with Buffalo Bill's Wild West show for more than fifteen years. Her relationship with William was one of trusted friendship. Drawn together by their similar rough upbringing and love of hunting and performing, the pair had a mutual respect and admiration for each other.[4] Annie noted in her biography that "there were hundreds of people in the outfit. . . . And the whole time we were one great family, loyal to one man, Buffalo Bill Cody. His words were better than most contracts."[5]

The demure entertainer's front-and-center spot in Buffalo Bill's show helped make the program a success but had a negative effect on his marriage. The attention he paid to Annie's career was threatening to Louisa. She was jealous of any woman who could take William's focus away from her and their children for any reason. Louisa didn't doubt that William and Annie's association was strictly platonic, but that didn't stop her from resenting the overly kind considerations her husband made for the sharpshooter.

Annie's relationship with William extended beyond one of employer and employee. During the off-season of the Wild West show, she and Frank Butler often visited the Codys at their ranch in Nebraska. Annie and Buffalo Bill thought of each other as siblings. They spent time together riding, roping, and practicing the art of shooting glass balls that were tossed into the air. In 1889 he gave her a high-spirited horse named Black Jack as a gift. Annie was one of only a few who could ride the once-wild horse, and William admired her fearlessness with the animal. He had the horse transported to Europe with the rest of the entourage for their overseas tour.[6]

In addition to Louisa's frustration over the generous gifts her husband gave the female cast member was the jealousy she felt over Annie's reputation. The public viewed Louisa as cold and somewhat distant. Annie, on the other hand, was

Scout's Rest Ranch, built in 1886 at North Platte, Nebraska, was a favorite vacation spot for many of Buffalo Bill Cody's Wild West show cast members.
Buffalo Bill Historical Center, Cody, WY, P.69.1344

revered by millions. "How I admired her," one female fan said after seeing Annie perform. "I would have given anything if I could rope and ride and shoot as she did."[7]

Louisa stayed largely removed from William's professional life and concentrated her attention on maintaining the home. Rarely, if ever, did she discuss the show or Annie Oakley with him, and he was not in the habit of divulging specifics about the acts or his business dealings. Her disinterest in his livelihood drove him to seek attention elsewhere. Annie served as his confidante on more than one occasion. She was not a drinker but could be persuaded to have a glass of wine with Buffalo Bill periodically. He would discuss upcoming performances, and they would exchange ideas for riding and shooting stunts.[8]

Annie's keen eye did not miss the many women who flirted with William and those he allowed to lead him astray. He wrote letters to Annie explaining why his attraction got the better of him and about his initial encounter with actress Katherine Clemmons. He eventually became romantically involved with Katherine, but in the beginning he was not impressed with her. "She is too swift and dishonest for me," he told Annie and Frank in a note dated January 27, 1891.[9]

The first year Annie was with Buffalo Bill's Wild West show, an elegant, high society lady sought to secure William's affections by signing up to join the cast. She thought it would be "cute to see the world from the back of a horse with Buffalo Bill." Life on the road proved to be more challenging than she anticipated, and in a short time any hope the woman had of remaining with the show dissipated. As Annie explained about the misguided woman in her autobiography,

> *A small tent with a cot was assigned her when she reached St. Louis. The next morning she stuck her head through the flap of the tent, spying a cowboy as he flitted by to slick up his mustache before the bugle blew for breakfast. She called out, "I say, you, where do I get my bath? There is only a pitcher of cold water here. Bring me some hot water quick." "I don't do that, Ma'am," the cowboy said. "Cody would never forgive me. He will attend to that honor himself, if you will convey a personal note for his perusal.*
>
> *So the note for her bath went forth. Cody opened and closed his mouth hard enough to unhinge his jaw. Then he joined the cowboy in a hearty laugh and ordered a small boy to take the lady a bucket of hot water.*

*In the first parade, the lady had to be lifted
from her mount after riding only a quarter of the
way around. She was on her way home that night,
cured of the idea that honest, hard work was "just
too cute."*[10]

At times Annie did empathize with Louisa's feelings of
jealousy. Annie was fond of William and supported him in
most matters, but she believed that Louisa's gruff, distant
behavior toward her husband was justified at times. Annie
struggled herself with wanting Buffalo Bill's undivided attention. When fourteen-year-old Lillian Smith was hired on with
the show in 1886 and billed as the "Champion Rifle Shot of
the World," Annie was resentful. She was the troupe's female
sharpshooting star and didn't care for the idea of another
woman encroaching on her territory. "Another joined the company," Annie wrote about Lillian in her memoirs, "bragging of
how Annie Oakley was done for once they saw her own self
shoot. Well, they saw both her work and her ample figure and
the next season her salary was cut in half."[11]

The ordinarily self-assured Annie would not allow herself
to be upstaged in either William's eyes or the audience's. In
between performances, she developed new acts designed not
only to challenge her own abilities but also to prove to William
that she was a better entertainer than Lillian. Buffalo Bill
never doubted Annie's exceptional showmanship. His motivation for adding a second female trick shooter was purely
financial. He wanted his program to be a commercial success.
Lillian had her followers, but Annie was the main attraction.
"[Annie] was a consummate actress," William bragged in a letter to his press agent, "with a personality that makes itself
felt as soon as she enters the arena. She is the single greatest
asset the Wild West Show ever had."[12]

William frequently told Annie how much she meant to
him and the show, but by early 1887 she felt as though she

Annie Oakley, or "Little Missie," as Buffalo Bill referred to her, with one of her beloved dogs, circa 1890
Buffalo Bill Historical Center, Cody, WY, P.69.1190

was being taken for granted. A great deal of time and money was being invested in promoting Lillian Smith. Annie Oakley was well known, but Lillian was a hopeful star whose name was not yet recognized. Wherever the show was based, William saturated the area with posters and flyers about Lillian. The publicity he created for her, borrowed in part from her life, claimed that when she was a little girl, she had traded her toys for a gun. "Tired of playing with dolls at the age of seven," William told the press, "she took up the rifle, shooting forty mallards and redheads a day on the wing and bobcats out of towering redwoods."[13]

The rivalry between Annie and Lillian was further fueled by William when he offered $10,000 to anyone who could publicly outshoot Lillian. Convinced that Lillian was getting far more attention than she was, Annie left the Wild West show in 1887. The only condition on which she would be persuaded to return was if Lillian were no longer with the program.

Lillian left the Buffalo Bill's Wild West cast in 1889 and formed her own short-lived show. A desperate struggle with alcohol and weight gain forced her to abandon her own show. Shortly after Lillian's entertainment career ended, Annie and William were appearing on the same bill again.

Annie enjoyed seventeen seasons with William's show. She retired from regularly performing in 1902.[14] The injuries she sustained in the 1901 train accident had caused trauma to her spine and made it too painful for her to continue riding.[15] On January 10, 1917, Annie was giving an exhibition of her shooting skills on the East Coast when she received the news that Buffalo Bill had died. Her tribute to the showman appeared in the newspaper he established, *The Cody Enterprise.*

He was the kindest, simplest, most loyal man I ever knew. He was the staunchest friend. He was in fact the personification of those sturdy and lovable qualities that really made the West and they were

the final criterion of all men. . . . His relations with
everyone he came in contact with were the most cor-
dial and trusting of any man I knew.[16]

Cody's Wild West show brought Annie Oakley and William Cody together as entertainers, and more than a decade of touring the globe with the program made them fast friends. Almost every account that has been written about their lives mention the significant impact they had on each other, both professionally and personally.

Annie's name is conspicuously absent from Louisa's biography. In an effort to keep one aspect of her life where her husband's name and Annie's were not intertwined, she chose to omit William's beloved "Missie" from her memoirs.

ELEVEN

The Final Ride

———▸•◂———

I wish to forget our tribulations and remember only the good in our union.

—William F. Cody, on his marriage to Louisa (1910)

On July 28, 1910, Irma Cody-Garlow nervously paced up and down the inlaid parquet floors outside the spacious library at her parents' home in North Platte. Welcome Wigwam was a large, ornate three-story house her father had purchased for the family in 1893. The structure was her mother's primary residence. A variety of guests had visited the grand home during the fifteen years Louisa lived there. Between theatrical seasons, William invited politicians, entertainers, and foreign dignitaries to stay at the Nebraska house. They could relax in their own private rooms, enjoy horseback riding across the wide-open countryside, and visit the museum on the third floor of the residence, which was filled with mementos Buffalo Bill had brought home from his travels.

William seldom spent any extended time at Welcome Wigwam. He preferred to stay at Scout's Rest Ranch, away from Louisa. She didn't object. The living arrangement had broadened the distance between them. The animosity the couple had for each other erupted into a public divorce hearing in 1905, leaving each of them with hurt feelings and lingering bitterness. Irma and her fourteen-year-old nephew, Cody Boal, who had been raised by Louisa since his mother Arta's death in 1904, were deeply affected by the ongoing strife. They made plans to trick Louisa and William into meeting with each other to iron out their differences once and for all.

Although the heavy door to the library was closed, Irma could make out the voices of her parents deep in discussion. At times the conversation seemed heated, but she resisted the temptation to interrupt their talk. For many years Irma had been the go-between for her parents. They refused to speak to each other directly and used their daughter to convey their requests, criticism, and plans. Irma disliked the uncomfortable position Louisa and William put her in, and it was in part the desire to remove herself from the situation and the dream of seeing her parents back together that prompted her to seek out a resolution.

After several hours the Codys emerged from the library reconciled. The only conditions they placed on each other was that William had to abstain from drinking (he had given it up nine years earlier) and that Louisa would accompany her husband to New York, where the Wild West show was set to open at Madison Square Garden.[1]

News of the restoration of the Codys' marriage reached the local newspaper, and an article congratulating the two appeared in the *North Platte Telegraph*. The owner-editor of the paper, A. P. Kelley, "wished Louisa and William many happy days together." The article also extended best wishes to Irma and the rest of the family.[2]

Throughout the course of the Codys' rocky relationship, Louisa had tried to persuade her daughters to side with her against William. Arta was prone to take her mother's position, but Irma favored her father no matter what he did. She enjoyed his company, and they shared similar interests. Both took pride in horses and riding, and they liked to entertain. Guests at William's home bragged that like her father, "Irma had the rare ability of making every guest feel they were the one most welcome."[3]

William F. Cody and his wife Louisa (1916)
Buffalo Bill Historical Center, Cody, WY, P.69.768

Irma and William had both experienced Louisa's quick temper. Indeed, all of the children were subject to Louisa's verbally abusive tirades at one time or another, but Irma had withstood physical abuse as well. When news of the severity of Louisa's actions came out in court during the divorce hearing, William was deeply saddened.[4] Irma and William also had the same response to Louisa's preoccupation with mediums. Both found it peculiar. During the divorce hearing, Louisa followed the medium's directives more closely than those of her lawyers. She put a lot of stock in her disturbing, nocturnal dreams and was addicted to Ouija boards.[5]

William overcompensated for Louisa's oddities and his frequent absences from home by showering his girls with presents. Educated at the best eastern schools, Arta and Irma were accustomed to the finest of everything. William made sure they got whatever they asked for—clothing, carriages, lavish parties. All his daughters needed to do was select an item, and it was theirs. In her younger years Irma traveled with her mother to Boston, where they spent time with many high society families. Louisa wanted her daughter to be influenced by wealthy, important people in business. She hoped their company would counteract the rough and rowdy influence the cast of the Wild West show had on Irma.[6]

Irma understood how driven her father was at his work and had grown familiar with his missing major events such as birthdays, baptisms, and holidays. When she married Lieutenant Clarence Armstrong Stott in February 1903, she was disappointed that William couldn't attend, but she understood that he was overseas performing. After the wedding she and her father wrote often, even when he was touring. Lieutenant Stott and Irma were stationed in China and the Philippines. Once Irma and her husband were transferred back to the United States, she made a point of visiting her father in Nebraska whenever he was there.

Fellow soldiers and neighbors of Irma and the lieutenant suggested that the Stotts had a troubled marriage. Much
like her father, there were rumors that Irma was not a faithful spouse. After only four years of marriage, Lieutenant Stott
became ill with pneumonia while on the job in White Horse,
South Dakota. He died on December 16, 1907.[7] Irma returned
to North Platte from the post in Iowa where they had been stationed. According to Julia Cody Goodman's memoirs, Irma was
distraught over her loss and sought the comfort of her father.
She traveled back and forth from Nebraska to Cody, Wyoming,
to visit William. Sometime during her frequent trips, Irma met
and married Frederick Garlow, the son of a prominent business
owner from Omaha.[8] Irma and Fred would go on to have three
children, two boys and a girl, whom her parents cherished.

For a few weeks the newlyweds accompanied William
and his cast of entertainers to various performance locations.
Buffalo Bill eventually made his son-in-law the manager of
Scout's Rest Ranch, and Irma and Fred settled in Nebraska.
In case his daughter got lonesome for him and wanted to visit,
William furnished her with a schedule of show dates and locations. He was always anxious to see Irma and show her around.
He found her easy to talk to and to be with because she wasn't
judgmental. Whenever the subject of Louisa and his marital
problems arose, William was highly respectful. "Your mother
wanted me all to herself; and that includes all friends of both
sexes," he said to Irma. "She would have been happiest if I had
found employment in Saint Louis and returned each evening
to her kitchen to spend time with her and the children."[9]

Despite the differences her parents had, Irma never stopped
believing that their marriage could be salvaged. Her fourteen-
year-old nephew, Cody, helped her arrange the meeting that
led to Louisa and Buffalo Bill being reunited. After more than
eight years leading separate lives, William sent a letter to his
wife asking to be "forgiven for the past." The tour the pair took

shortly after making up included stops in Pennsylvania, Montana, and the Southwest. "We've had peaceful and loving trips together," William recalled some time later in Nebraska. "In the past four years, we've traveled to Oracle, Arizona, together and she loves to read or knit on the veranda of our country inn while I look after our mining interests. She's less of a homebody now that the children are grown and gone."[10]

Ecstatic that her parents' union had withstood many trials and troubles, Irma made plans to celebrate the couple's forty-fifth wedding anniversary. A great deal had happened since Louisa and William's reconciliation.

The anniversary festivities were held over a two-day period at the Codys' ranch in North Platte. The twenty-six guests, including Louisa's divorce attorney and his wife, were treated to a seven-course meal served at a lavishly set table with fresh flowers, cut glass, and silver. "I have forgotten all our tribulations," William told their friends, "and remember only the good in our union." When reflecting on Louisa's past unpleasant behavior toward guests at Scout's Rest Ranch, he said that there had been "much misunderstanding. But all is forgiven."[11]

A month after the anniversary party, William began the farewell tour of his Wild West show. He would again be gone from Louisa for long periods of time. She was used to the lifestyle and made no issue of his going. "Now our marriage had a few bad patches," he recalled years later, "and these are public record and no more needs to be said of them. But I want to tell you that no man was more blessed in his wedlock than I and I have the fondest regard for Lulu."[12]

William's later years were spent negotiating peace between his sisters more so than between himself and Louisa. May, Helen, and Julia were jealous not only of one another at times but also of Louisa and Irma, as well as the men and women in Cody's life whom he tried to help financially. When

Margaret Louisa Frederici Cody, 1843–1921
Buffalo Bill Historical Center, Cody, WY, P.6.302

the infighting and malicious talk about whatever was bothering them became too much, William, as usual, would turn to Julia for help and a sympathetic ear. In a letter to Julia in October 1905, he expressed his exasperation with his sister's behavior. He wrote,

> *Julia Dear, I can't stand it. Nellie no sooner gets back to Cody. And listens to gossip, then jumps on me with a ten page letter accusing me of everything vile. Says I have left you with a mortgaged house on your old shoulders. Will you please give her the facts, before she tells it all over town. She says I spend thousands of dollars more on others than I do on my sisters.*[13]

Before Irma helped her parents reconcile, Louisa complained to her youngest daughter that William spent much more money on his sisters than he did on his wife and children. Irma disagreed and championed her father's giving nature to both her mother and her aunts. Irma kept William apprised of the disparaging talk whenever she went to see him. He listened and then encouraged his daughter to "ignore the lot of them." Buffalo Bill looked forward to being with Irma. Often she would meet him at the train depot to welcome him home. He would put his arm around her, and they would walk side by side talking until they reached their final destination.[14]

As her father got older, Irma worried about his declining health. William suffered from inflammation of the joints and was constantly uncomfortable. In May 1910 he announced his plans to retire and enjoy some of the fruits of his labor. However, he was not ready to give up the spotlight until the winter of 1916. At the age of sixty-nine, he was exhausted and in extreme pain from acute arthritis. He had to be helped in and out of his saddle before and after each performance. His last show was on November 11, 1916, at Portsmouth, Virginia. When the program ended, the crowd gave the tearful Buffalo Bill Cody a ten-minute standing ovation.

Shortly after his final public ride, William headed to Colorado to visit his sister May. No sooner had he arrived than he became seriously ill. Telegrams were quickly sent to Louisa, Irma, Fred, and Julia summoning them to his bedside. The December 17, 1916, edition of the *San Francisco Examiner* claimed that Buffalo Bill was suffering from a general breakdown. Within a few days his health briefly improved. "You can't kill the old scout," William told his physician whenever his condition started to get better.[15]

His family was so convinced he was on his way to a full recovery that they returned to their homes. A few weeks later they rushed back to Denver after receiving word that William had had a relapse. He was then taken to the Glenwood Springs resort in the hope that treatment at the facility might help him get better, but his condition didn't change.

In her autobiography, Louisa recalled how hard William fought to stay alive and how he comforted her when she thought the end was near. "He laughed at my tears, he patted my cheek, and strove to assemble again the old, booming voice. But it was weak and now breaking," she noted. "'Don't worry, Momma,' he said time after time. 'I'm going to be all right. The doctor says I'm going to die, does he? Well, I'm pretty much alive just now, ain't I. I've still got my boots on. I'll be all right.'"[16]

According to Irma, when the doctor told William his life was ebbing, "he accepted his fate like a stoic." He told Julia to "let the Elks and Masons take charge of the funeral." He then made arrangements with his relatives regarding his business affairs, urging them to continue his work.[17]

On January 9, 1917, William slipped into a coma. He died the following morning from acute cardiac trouble, hypertension, and kidney failure. News of Buffalo Bill's passing echoed around the globe. His wife and daughter were showered with condolences from kings, military leaders, and politicians. Historians

STATE OF COLORADO
Bureau of Vital Statistics
Certificate of Death

1 PLACE OF DEATH

County __Denver__   File No. __187__

Town __"__   Registration District No. _____   Registered No. _____

or City __"__   No. __2932 Lafayette__ _____St,_____Ward
(If death occurred in a hospital or institution, give its name instead of street and number)

2 FULL NAME __William F. Cody__

(a) Residence. No. __Wyoming__ _____St,_____Ward. _____
(Usual place of abode)   (If nonresident give city or town and State)
(b) Length of residence in city or town where death occurred   yrs. __1__ mos.   ds.   How long in U. S., if of foreign birth ?   yrs.   mos.   ds.

PERSONAL AND STATISTICAL PARTICULARS				MEDICAL CERTIFICATE OF DEATH
3 SEX	**4 COLOR OR RACE**	**5** Single, Married, Widowed, or Divorced (write the word)		**16 DATE OF DEATH** (month, day and year)
Male	White	Married		Jan. 10 1917

5a If married, widowed or divorced
HUSBAND of
(or) WIFE of

6 DATE OF BIRTH (month, day, and year)
__Feb. 26. 1846__

7 AGE	Years	Months	Days	IF LESS than
	70	10	15	1 day, ____hrs. or ____min.

17 I HEREBY CERTIFY, That I attended deceased from __Dec. 14__, 19__16__ to __Jan. 10__, 19__17__
that I last saw h__im__ alive on __Jan. 10__, 1917, and
that death occurred, on the date stated above, at __12:05p__ m.
The CAUSE of DEATH* was as follows:

__Uremic Poisoning__

8 OCCUPATION OF DECEASED
(a) Trade, profession, or particular kind of work __Showman__
(b) General nature of industry, business, or establishment in which employed (or employer) _____
(c) Name of employer _____

_____(duration) ____yrs. ____mos. ____ds.
CONTRIBUTORY
(Secondary)
_____(duration) ____yrs. ____mos. ____ds.

9 BIRTHPLACE (city or town) _____
(State or country) __Iowa__

18 Where was disease contracted
if not at place of death? __Colo.__
Did an operation precede death? _____ Date of _____
Was there an autopsy? _____
What test confirmed diagnosis? _____
(Signed) __J. H. East__ _____, M. D.

10 NAME OF FATHER __I. Cody__
11 BIRTHPLACE OF FATHER
(City or town) _____
(State or country) __Canada__
12 MAIDEN NAME OF MOTHER __Mary B. Laycock__
13 BIRTHPLACE OF MOTHER
(City or town) _____
(State or country) __Penna.__

__Jan.11,17__ (Address) __1510 Glenarm__
*State the Disease Causing Death, or in deaths from Violent Causes, state (1) Means and Nature of Injury, and (2) whether Accidental, Suicidal, or Homicidal. (See reverse side for additional space.)

14 Informant __Mrs. Louisa M. Cody__
(Address) __2932 Lafayette__

19 PLACE OF BURIAL, CREMATION, OR REMOVAL | **DATE OF BURIAL**
__Olinger Vault__ | __Jan. 14__ 19__17__

15 Filed __1-12__, 19__17__ __Sherman__
Registrar.

20 UNDERTAKER | **ADDRESS**
__Olinger__ | __2600-16th__

hereby certify that on June 3, 1917, The Olinger Mortuary removed from the vault
d buried on Lookout Mountain the body of deceased named in above report after receiving written permission from local registrar. F. W. Farmer.

STATE OF COLORADO, ss. Subscribed and sworn to before me a Notary
Public this June 24, 1927. Agnes Ellis
My commission expires October 5, 1929. SEAL.

I, __S. R. McKelvey__, State Registrar of Vital

Statistics of the State of Colorado, do hereby certify that the above is a

true, full and correct copy of the original death certificate of _____

__William F. Cody__

in my custody and now on file in my office.

WITNESS my hand and official seal at Denver, in said State, this

__24th__ day of __June__ A. D. 19 __27__

S. R. McKelvey
State Registrar of Vital Statistics.

Deputy State Registrar of Vital

Certificate of Death for William F. Cody
Buffalo Bill Historical Center Cody, WY, MS 6 Series IV Box 4 Folder 10

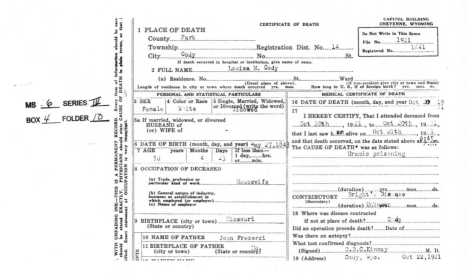

Certificate of Death for Louisa Cody, front
Buffalo Bill Historical Center Cody, WY, MS 6 Series IV Box 4 Folder 10

paid tribute to William in newspapers and referred to him as "the finest specimen of young manhood in the West."[18] Reporters at *Hearst Magazine* called Buffalo Bill the "last of the vanished Wild West's heroes." In a series of articles about the showman, *Hearst Magazine* editors noted that with William's passing "disappeared the one great vivid personality which remained as a living link between the present generations and the courageous founders of that now rich and civilized American empire that was the 'Wild West.'"[19]

The days leading to William's funeral were a haze for his family and close friends. Before being buried at Lookout Mountain in Denver, his body lay in state at the capitol building. Throngs of sorrowful fans passed by to view Buffalo Bill and pay respects to their idol. Louisa and Julia disagreed about where William's remains were to rest. Julia insisted that he had picked Cedar Mountain in Cody as his favored spot to be buried, and his will confirmed that wish. Louisa said that William had changed his mind and asked her to bury him in

REVISED UNITED STATES STANDARD CERTIFICATE OF DEATH

(Approved by U. S. Census and American Public Health Association.)

Statement of occupation.—Precise statement of occupation is very important, so that the relative healthfulness of various pursuits can be known. The question applies to each and every person, irrespective of age. For many occupations a single word or term on the first line will be sufficient, e. g., Farmer or Planter, Physician, Compositor, Architect, Locomotive engineer, Civil engineer, Stationary fireman, etc. But in many cases, especially in industrial employments, it is necessary to know (a) the kind of work and also (b) the nature of the business or industry, and therefore an additional line is provided for the later statement; it should be used only when needed. As examples: (a) Spinner, (b) Cotton mill; (a) Salesman, (b) Grocery; (a) Foreman, (b) Automobile factory. The material worked on may form part of the second statement. Never return "Laborer," "Foreman," "Manager," "Dealer," etc., without more precise specification, as Day laborer, Farm laborer, Laborer—Coal mine, etc. Women at home, who are engaged in the duties of the household only (not paid Housekeepers who receive a definite salary), may be entered as Housewife, Housework, or At home, and children, not gainfully employed, as At school or At home. Care should be taken to report specifically the occupations of persons engaged in domestic service for wages, as Servant, Cook, Housemaid, etc. If the occupation has been changed or given up on account of the Disease Causing Death, state occupation at beginning of illness. If retired from business, that fact may be indicated thus: Farmer (retired, 6 yrs.). For persons who have no occupation whatever, write None.

Statement of cause of death.—Name, first, the Disease Causing Death (the primary affection with respect to time and causation), using always the same accepted term for the disease. Example: Cerebrospinal fever (the only definite synonym is "Epidemic cerebrospinal meningitis"); Diphtheria (avoid use of "Croup"); Typhoid fever (never report "Typhoid pneumonia"); Lobar pneumonia; Bronchopneumonia ("Pneumonia," unqualified, is indefinite; Tuberculosis of lungs, meninges, peritoneum, etc., Carcinoma, Sarcoma, etc., of................ (name origin; "Cancer" is less definite; avoid use of "Tumor" for malignant neoplasms); Measles; Whooping cough; Chronic valvular heart disease; Chronic interstitial nephritis, etc. The contributory (secondary or intercurrent) affection need not be stated unless important. Example: Measles (disease causing death), 29 ds.; Bronchopneumonia (secondary), 10 ds. Never report mere symptoms or terminal conditions, such as "Asthenia," "Anemia," (merely symptomatic), "Atrophy," "Col-

lapse," "Coma," "Convulsions," "Debility" ("Congenital," "Senile," etc.), "Dropsy," "Exhaustion," "Heart failure," "Hemorrhage," "Inanition," "Marasmus," "Old age," "Shock," "Uremia," "Weakness," etc., when a definite disease can be ascertained as the cause. Always qualify all diseases resulting from childbirth or miscarriage, as "Puerperal septicemia," "Puerperal peritonitis," etc. State cause for which surgical operation was undertaken. For Violent Deaths state Means of Injury and qualify as Accidental, Suicidal, or Homicidal, or as probably such, is impossible to determine definitely. Examples: Accidental drowning; Struck by railway train—accident; Revolver wound of head—homicide; Poisoned by carbolic acid—probably suicide. The nature of the injury, as fracture of skull, and consequences (e. g., sepsis, tetanus) may be stated under the head of "Contributory." (Recommendations on statement of cause of death approved by Committee on Nomenclature of the American Medical Association.)

NOTE—Individual offices may add to above list of undesirable terms and refuse to accept certificates containing them. Thus the form in use in New York City states: "Certificates will be returned for additional information which give any of the following diseases, without explanation, as the sole cause of death: Abortion, cellulitis, childbirth, convulsions, hemorrhage, gangrene, gastritis, erysipelas, meningitis, miscarriage, necrosis, peritonitis, phlebitis, pyemia, septicemia, tetanus." But general adoption of the minimum list suggested will work vast improvement, and its scope can be extended at a later date.

Additional Space for Further Statements by Physician.

STATE OF WYOMING, ss:

I, W.H.Hassed, M.D., State Registrar of Vital Statistics of the State of Wyoming, do hereby certify that the reverse is a full true and correct copy of the original death certificate of

LOUISA M. CODY

in my custody and now on file in my office.

WITNESS my hand and official seal at Cheyenne, in said State, this 20th. day of June A.D. 1927.

W. H. Hassed, M.D.
State Registrar of Vital Statistic

Certificate of Death for Louisa Cody, back
Buffalo Bill Historical Center Cody, WY, MS 6 Series IV Box 4 Folder 10

Colorado. "It's pretty up there," Louisa wrote he told her on his deathbed. "I want to be buried up there instead of Wyoming."[20] The road to the site in Colorado was snow-covered, and it was six months before William's grave could be dug. Thousands of mourners followed the flag-draped casket up to the mountain grave the day of his funeral. Among the tearful grievers were six unidentified women, rumored to have been romantically involved with Buffalo Bill.[21]

William made provisions in his will for Julia, May, and their families (Helen had preceded him in death) and for Irma and her family, but the bulk of his estate, valued at more than $65,000, went to Louisa.

Louisa returned to Wyoming with Irma, Fred, and their three children after the memorial service. Irma and her husband managed the hotel William had built in Cody and also helped to care for his other properties there. In October 1918 the couple both came down with the flu and died within four days of each other. Irma was thirty-four years old. Heartbroken, Louisa assumed the responsibility of raising her grandchildren. She lamented the loss of her family in her autobiography, published in 1919. "I face the sunset," she observed. "My children are gone. . . . I am alone, my life lived, my hands folded. . . . It will not be long now until I see the fading of the sunset in my own little world, until the time shall come when I am with the children I loved, and the man I loved—on the trail beyond."[22]

Mrs. William Cody passed away on October 20, 1921, from heart disease. Louisa wanted to be buried with Buffalo Bill, but William's sister told the *Denver Post* that the request "could not be realized."

"It would be necessary to blast the grave out of solid rock," May Decker shared with reporters. "This could not be done without great damage to Colonel Cody's burial place." Louisa's attorney helped make it possible for her to be buried in the grave with William without harming the site. On November 1, 1921, her body was placed above the concrete layer that covered William's coffin.[23]

William was seventy years old when he died. Louisa was seventy-eight. Their turbulent marriage lasted more than fifty years.

NOTES

Introduction

1. Joy Kasson, *Buffalo Bill's Wild West* (New York: Hill & Wang, 2000), 36.
2. William F. Cody, *The Adventures of Buffalo Bill* (New York: Harper & Row Publishers, 1904), 139.
3. Nellie Snyder Yost, *Buffalo Bill: His Family, Friends, Fame, Failures, and Fortunes* (Chicago: Sage Books, 1979), 99.
4. *Cody v. Cody* deposition, District County of Sheridan County, Wyoming, February–April 1904, 11.
5. Julia Cody Goodman and Elizabeth Leonard, *Buffalo Bill: King of the Old West* (New York: Library Publishers, 1955), 142.
6. Larry McMurtry, *The Colonel and Little Missie* (New York: Simon & Schuster, 2005), 110–111; *New York Times*, October 30, 1898; Yost, *Buffalo Bill*, 99.
7. Don Russell, *The Lives and Legends of Buffalo Bill Cody* (Norman: University of Oklahoma Press, 1979), 258.
8. William F. Cody, *An Autobiography of Buffalo Bill* (New York: Cosmopolitan Book, 1920), 5–6.
9. Ibid., 15.
10. Ibid., 118.
11. Yost, *Buffalo Bill*, 71.
12. Ibid.

One: Man of the Family

1. William F. Cody, *The Adventures of Buffalo Bill* (New York: Harper & Row Publishers, 1904), 120; Helen Cody Wetmore, *Last of the Great Scouts* (Chicago: Duluth Press, 1899), 58–59.
2. Julia Cody Goodman and Elizabeth Leonard, *Buffalo Bill: King of the Old West* (New York: Library Publishers, 1955), 75; Cody, *The Adventures of Buffalo Bill*, 122.
3. Helen Cody Wetmore, *Last of the Great Scouts* (Chicago: Duluth Press Publishing, 1899), xiii.

4. Goodman and Leonard, *Buffalo Bill*, 38.

5. Wetmore, *Last of the Great Scouts*, 3.

6. Cody, *The Adventures of Buffalo Bill*, 101.

7. William F. Cody, *An Autobiography of Buffalo Bill* (New York: Cosmopolitan Book, 1920), 6; Goodman and Leonard, *Buffalo Bill*, 73.

8. Adolph Regli, *The Real Book about Buffalo Bill* (New York: Garden City Books, 1952), 30; Goodman and Leonard, *Buffalo Bill*, 307.

9. Wetmore, *Last of the Great Scouts*, 11.

10. Cody, *An Autobiography of Buffalo Bill*, 15.

11. Wetmore, *Last of the Great Scouts*, 40–43.

12. Cody, *An Autobiography of Buffalo Bill*, 29.

13. Wetmore, *Last of the Great Scouts*, 47.

14. Ibid., 101.

15. Don Russell, *The Lives and Legends of Buffalo Bill* (Norman: University of Oklahoma, 1979), 17.

16. Buffalo Bill Historical Center McCracken Research Library, MS6, 1B, Box 1, Folder 5.

17. Ibid.

18. "Buffalo Bill Cody," Wikipedia, www.wikipedia.com.

19. Nellie Snyder Yost, *Buffalo Bill: His Family, Friends, Fame, Failures, and Fortunes* (Chicago: Sage Books, 1979), 226.

20. Ibid., 43.

21. Wetmore, *Last of the Great Scouts*, 175.

22. Ibid., 123.

23. Goodman and Leonard, *Buffalo Bill*, 138.

24. Ibid., 139; Louisa Cody and Courtney Ryley Cooper, *Memories of Buffalo Bill* (New York: D. Appleton, 1919), 36.

25. Goodman and Leonard, *Buffalo Bill*, 138–139.

26. Wetmore, *Last of the Great Scouts*, 132.

Two: The Courtship of Louisa

1. Joy Kasson, *Buffalo Bill's Wild West* (New York: Hill & Wang, 2000), 18–19.

2. Helen Cody Wetmore, *Last of the Great Scouts* (Chicago: Duluth Press Publishing, 1899), 122.

3. William F. Cody, *An Autobiography of Buffalo Bill* (New York: Cosmopolitan Book, 1920), 90–91.

4. "Louisa Frederici," Arnold Historical Society, www .arnoldhistorical.org, 2–4.

5. Wetmore, *Last of the Great Scouts*, 122.

6. Nellie Snyder Yost, *Buffalo Bill: His Family, Friends, Fame, Failures, and Fortunes* (Chicago: Sage Books, 1979), 10–11; Louisa Cody and Courtney Ryley Cooper, *Memories of Buffalo Bill* (New York: D. Appleton, 1919), 34.

7. Cody and Cooper, *Memories of Buffalo Bill*, 5.

8. Ibid., 9–11; Adolph Regli, *The Real Book about Buffalo Bill* (New York: Garden City Books, 1952), 124–125.

9. Julia Cody Goodman and Elizabeth Leonard, *Buffalo Bill: King of the Old West* (New York: Library Publishers, 1955), 137.

10. Cody, *An Autobiography of Buffalo Bill*, 94.

11. Ibid., 95.

12. Ibid., 91–100; Wetmore, *Last of the Great Scouts*, 134.

13. Cody and Cooper, *Memories of Buffalo Bill*, 42–44.

14. Regli, *The Real Book about Buffalo Bill*, 125–126.

15. Cody, *An Autobiography of Buffalo Bill*, 99–101.

16. Ibid., 104.

17. Ibid., 105.

18. Cody and Cooper, *Memories of Buffalo Bill*, 67–68.

THREE: Husband, Father, Scout, and Actor

1. Nellie Snyder Yost, *Buffalo Bill: His Family, Friends, Fame, Failures, and Fortunes* (Chicago: Sage Books, 1979), 18.

2. Louisa Cody and Courtney Ryley Cooper, *Memories of Buffalo Bill* (New York: D. Appleton, 1919), 155–157.

3. William F. Cody, *An Autobiography of Buffalo Bill* (New York: Cosmopolitan Book, 1920), 137–140; Adolph Regli, *The Real Book about Buffalo Bill* (New York: Garden City Books, 1952), 141; Yost, *Buffalo Bill*, 4.

4. Julia Cody Goodman and Elizabeth Leonard, *Buffalo Bill: King of the Old West* (New York: Library Publishers, 1955), 188; William Cody, *The Adventures of Buffalo Bill* (New York: Harper & Brothers, 1904), 135.

5. Regli, *The Real Book about Buffalo Bill*, 160.

6. Yost, *Buffalo Bill*, 40.

7. Cody and Cooper, *Memories of Buffalo Bill*, 196–205.

8. Ibid., 160–164.

9. Goodman and Leonard, *Buffalo Bill*, 195–196; Yost, *Buffalo Bill*, 25; William F. Cody, *Buffalo Bill's Life Story* (New York: Cosmopolitan Book, 1920), 159.

10. Jay Monaghan, *The Great Rascal: The Life and Adventures of Ned Buntline* (New York: Bantam Book, 1953), 4.

11. Yost, *Buffalo Bill*, 45.

12. Cody and Cooper, *Memories of Buffalo Bill*, 207.

13. Henry E. Davies and Paul A. Hutton, *Ten Days on the Plains* (Dallas: Southern Methodist University, 1985), 25–26.

14. Cody and Cooper, *Memories of Buffalo Bill*, 218.

15. Don Russell, *The Lives and Legends of Buffalo Bill Cody* (Norman: University of Oklahoma Press, 1979), 182.

16. Cody and Cooper, *Memories of Buffalo Bill*, 221.

17. Ibid., 232.

18. Ibid., 231.

Four: Life in the Limelight

1. Helen Cody Wetmore, *Last of the Great Scouts* (Chicago: Duluth Press Publishing, 1899), 211.

2. Ibid., 211.

3. Buffalo Bill Historical Center McCraken Research Library, MS6, IB, Box 1, Folder 5.

4. Louisa Cody and Courtney Ryley Cooper, *Memories of Buffalo Bill* (New York: D. Appleton, 1919), 261–264.

5. Julia Cody Goodman and Elizabeth Leonard, *Buffalo Bill: King of the Old West* (New York: Library Publishers, 1955), 226.

6. *Cody v. Cody* deposition, District County of Sheridan County, Wyoming, February–April 1904, 29.

7. William F. Cody, *The Story of the Wild West: Buffalo Bill's Autobiography with Campfire Chats* (Waynesboro, TN: Historical Publication, 1888), 614.

8. Buffalo Bill Historical Center McCraken Research Library, MS6, IB, Box 1, Folder 5.

9. Cody, *The Story of the Wild West: Buffalo Bill's Autobiography with Campfire Chats*, 652; Cody and Cooper, *Memories of Buffalo Bill*, 251–252.

10. *Cody v. Cody* deposition, 3.

11. Ibid., 7.

12. Buffalo Bill Historical Center McCraken Research Library, MS6, IB, Box 1, Folder 5.

13. Cody and Cooper, *Memories of Buffalo Bill*, 267–270.

14. Adolph Regli, *The Real Book about Buffalo Bill* (New York: Garden City Books, 1952), 182.

15. *Cody v. Cody* deposition, 34.

16. Cody and Cooper, *Memories of Buffalo Bill*, 280.

17. Ibid., 281.

18. *Cody v. Cody* deposition, 13.

19. Ibid.

20. Ibid., 81.

21. Buffalo Bill Historical Center McCraken Research Library, MS6, IB, Box 1, Folder 5.

22. Cody, *William F. Buffalo Bill the Famous Hunter.*

23. Letter to Julia from William Cody Albany, New York, March 9, 1882.

24. Buffalo Bill Historical Center McCraken Research Library, MS6, IB, Box 1, Folder 6.

25. North Platte Telegraph, June 7, 1952; Nellie Snyder Yost, *Buffalo Bill: His Family, Friends, Fame, Failures, and Fortunes* (Chicago: Sage Books, 1979), 43.

26. Cody and Cooper, *Memories of Buffalo Bill*, 290.

27. Ibid.
28. Letter to Julia and Al from William Cody, Youngstown, Ohio, September 24, 1883.
29. Goodman and Leonard, *Buffalo Bill,* 237-239.
30. Wetmore, *Last of the Great Scouts,* 180.

FIVE: The Dear Favorite

1. Letter from William F. Cody to Mollie Moses, McCraken Research Library, MS6, IB, Box 1, 1886.
2. *The Evansville (Ind.) Press*, June 11, 1927.
3. Nellie Snyder Yost, *Buffalo Bill: His Family, Friends, Fame, Failures, and Fortunes* (Chicago: Sage Books, 1979), 141.
4. Ibid.
5. *The Evansville (Ind.) Press*, June 11, 1927.
6. Letter from William F. Cody to Mollie Moses, McCraken Research Library, MS6, IB, Box 1, November 1885.
7. Ibid., April 1886.
8. Ibid., March 1886.
9. Ibid., April 1886.
10. *The Evansville (Ind.) Press*, June 11, 1927.
11. Letter from William F. Cody to Mollie Moses, McCraken Research Library, MS6, Series IB, Box 1, November 1885.
12. Ibid., March 1886.
13. *The Evansville (Ind.) Press*, June 11, 1927.

SIX: Away from Home

1. "Colonel Cody Talks," *New York Recorder*, May 22, 1894.
2. Charles Musser, *Edison Motion Pictures, 1890–1900* (Washington, DC: Smithsonian Institution Press, 1997), 125–145; Julia Cody and Elizabeth Leonard, *Buffalo Bill: King of the Old West* (New York: Library Publishers, 1955), 263.
3. Louisa Cody and Courtney Ryley Cooper, *Memories of Buffalo Bill* (New York: D. Appleton, 1919), 290.
4. Nate Salsbury, *American Exhibition,* c. 1901, Buffalo Bill Historical Center Nate Salsbury Papers, Box 2, Folder 64.

5. *Cody v. Cody* deposition, District County of Sheridan County, Wyoming, February–April 1904, 32–33.

6. Ibid., 33.

7. Ibid., 45.

8. Ibid., 14–16.

9. Ibid.

10. Ibid.

11. Letter from William F. Cody to Al Goodman, Buffalo Bill Historical Center, McCraken Research Library, MS6, IIC, Box 1, Folder 5, August 1891.

12. Letter from Ed Goodman to Al and Julia Goodman, Buffalo Bill Historical Center, McCraken Research Library, MS6, IIC, Box 1, Folder 5, April 1887.

13. *Cody v. Cody* deposition, 30–35.

14. *Billings Gazette*, December 18, 1979, 14.

15. Ibid.; *Cody v. Cody* deposition, 32–33.

16. Ibid.

17. Ibid., 34.

18. Cody and Cooper, *Memories of Buffalo Bill,* 269.

19. Ibid., 299.

20. Stella Foote, *Letters from Buffalo Bill* (Billings, MT: Foote Publishing, 1954), 40.

21. *Chicago Post*, June 18, 1893.

22. Nellie Snyder Yost, *Buffalo Bill: His Family, Friends, Fame, Failures, and Fortunes* (Chicago: Sage Books, 1979), 276.

23. Letter from William Cody to Al and Julia Goodman, Buffalo Bill Historical Center, McCraken Research Library, MS6, IIC, Box 1, Folder 5, April 11, 1895.

24. Helen Cody Wetmore, *Last of the Great Scouts* (Chicago: Duluth Press Publishing, 1899), 282.

25. Ibid., xiii.

26. *North Platte Telegraph*, February 23, 1905; *Billings Gazette*, December 18, 1979, 14.

27. *Cody v. Cody* deposition, 43.

28. Ibid., 38.

SEVEN: The Lady of Venice

1. Isabelle S. Sayers, *Annie Oakley and Buffalo Bill's Wild West* (Toronto: General Publishing, 1981), 49–51; Dan Muller, *My Life with Buffalo Bill* (Chicago: Reilly & Lee, 1948), 432.

2. Muller, *My Life with Buffalo Bill*, 433.

3. Joy S. Kasson, *Buffalo Bill's Wild West: Celebrity, Memory, and Popular History* (New York: Hill & Wang, 2000), 138; *Covington Sun Newspaper*, April 16, 1908, 1.

4. 1870 United States Federal Census, Viola Clemmons; www.ancestory.com, Viola Katherine Clemmons.

5. Sayers, *Annie Oakley and Buffalo Bill's Wild West*, 49–51.

6. Kathryn Wright, "Buffalo Bill's Telegrams," *Billings Gazette Sunday Magazine*, February 22, 1976, 1, 3.

7. Ibid.

8. Ibid.

9. Ibid.

10. *Nebraska State Journal*, April 22, 1894, 13.

11. Ibid.

12. Larry McMurtry, *The Colonel and Little Missie* (New York: Simon & Schuster, 2006), 204; *New York Press*, October 30, 1898.

13. *Covington Sun Newspaper*, April 16, 1908, 1.

14. Ibid.

15. *New York Times*, June 11, 1909, 16.

16. *New York Times*, January 14, 1947, 27; Don Russell, *The Lives and Legends of Buffalo Bill Cody* (Norman: University of Oklahoma Press, 1979), 433.

EIGHT: The Cody Trials

1. Helen Cody Wetmore, *Last of the Great Scouts* (Chicago: Duluth Press Publishing, 1899), 266.

2. Chris Enss, *Buffalo Gals: Women of Buffalo Bill's Wild West Show* (Guilford, CT: Globe Pequot Press, 2006), 89–94.

3. *North Platte Semi Weekly Tribune,* March 20, 1899.

4. *New York Times*, December 25, 1902.
5. *North Platte Independent*, February 26, 1903.
6. Letter from William F. Cody to Julia Goodman, Buffalo Bill Historical Center, McCraken Research Library, MS6, IIC, Box 1, Folder 5, December 29, 1902.
7. Ibid.
8. *Chicago Daily Tribune*, February 17, 1905.
9. Letter from William F. Cody to Julia Goodman, Buffalo Bill Historical Center, McCraken Research Library, MS6, IIC, Box 1, Folder 5, July 1903.
10. *Rocky Mountain News*, July 23, 1970.
11. Nellie Snyder Yost, *Buffalo Bill: His Family, Friends, Fame, Failures, and Fortunes* (Chicago: Sage Books, 1979), 320.
12. *North Platte Telegraph*, January 1, 1870.
13. *Billings Gazette*, December 18, 1979.
14. *Denver Post*, April 22, 1904.
15. *Cripple Creek Times*, February 14, 1905.
16. *Billings Gazette*, December 18, 1979.
17. *Cody v. Cody* deposition, District County of Sheridan County, Wyoming, February–April 1904, 50–62.
18. Ibid.
19. Ibid.
20. Ibid.
21. *Billings Gazette*, December 18, 1979.
22. Ibid.
23. *Denver Post*, February 28, 1905.
24. *Cody v. Cody* deposition, 33–34.
25. *Chicago Daily Tribune*, January 8, 1954; *Cody v. Cody* deposition, 45.
26. *Cody v. Cody* deposition, 45.
27. Ibid., 16.
28. Ibid., 45-52.
29. Ibid.; *North Platte Telegraph*, June 1, 1905.
30. *Cody v. Cody* deposition, 16.

31. Ibid.

32. *Chicago Daily Tribune*, February 17, 1905.

33. Letter from William F. Cody to Julia Goodman, Buffalo Bill Historical Center, McCraken Research Library, MS6, IIC, Box 1, Folder 5, June 14, 1905.

34. Yost, *Buffalo Bill*, 335.

NINE: **A Wandering Heart**

1. *Cody v. Cody* deposition, District County of Sheridan County, Wyoming, February–April 1905, 7–9.

2. *Denver Post*, February 28, 1905.

3. *Frontier Times Magazine*, October 1926, 4–6.

4. *Cody v. Cody* deposition, 6–15.

5. Julia Cody Goodman and Elizabeth Leonard, *Buffalo Bill: King of the Old West* (New York: Library Publishers, 1955), 268.

6. Kristine Haglund, *Buffalo Bill Cody Country* (New York: Bison Book, 1975), 43.

7. *Cody v. Cody deposition*, 6–15.

8. Ibid., 7–9.

9. Ibid.

10. *New York Herald*, February 3, 1901; Albert Johannsen, *The House of Beadle & Adams* (Norman: University of Oklahoma Press, 1950), 187.

11. Johannsen, *The House of Beadle & Adams*, 187.

12. *North Platte Telegraph,* February 23, 1905.

13. Don Russell, *The Life of Honorable William F. Cody: Known as Buffalo Bill, the Famous Hunter, Scout, and Guide* (New York: Bison Book, 1978), 434–436.

14. *Cody v. Cody* deposition, 57.

TEN: **The Sharpshooter**

1. Isabelle Sayers, *Annie Oakley and Buffalo Bill's Wild West* (New York: Dover Publications, 1981), 23.

2. Annie Oakley, *The Story of My Life* (Greenville, OH: Darke County Historical Society, 1926), 22.
3. Julia Cody Goodman and Elizabeth Leonard, *Buffalo Bill: King of the Old West* (New York: Library Publishers, 1955), 239–240.
4. Joy Kasson, *Buffalo Bill's Wild West* (New York: Hill & Wang, 2000), 8.
5. Oakley, *The Story of My Life*, 12.
6. Don Russell, *The Lives and Legends of Buffalo Bill Cody* (Norman: University of Oklahoma Press, 1979), 321, 332; Nellie Snyder Yost, *Buffalo Bill: His Family, Friends, Fame, Failures, and Fortunes* (Chicago: Sage Books, 1979), 228.
7. Yost, *Buffalo Bill*, 274.
8. Kasson, *Buffalo Bill's Wild West*, 136; Larry McMurtry, *The Colonel and Little Missie* (New York: Simon & Schuster, 2005), 172.
9. Sayers, *Annie Oakley and Buffalo Bill's Wild West*, 49–50.
10. Oakley, *The Story of My Life*, 26.
11. Ibid., 18.
12. Glenn Shirley, "Lillian Smith: Bill Cody's California Girl," *Real West Magazine*, April 1973.
13. Goodman and Leonard, *Buffalo Bill*, 271.
14. Ibid.
15. Oakley, *The Story of My Life*, 22.
16. *The Cody Enterprise*, January 20, 1917.

ELEVEN: The Final Ride

1. Nellie Snyder Yost, *Buffalo Bill: His Family, Friends, Fame, Failures, and Fortunes* (Chicago: Sage Books, 1979), 362–364.
2. Don Russell, *The Lives and Legends of Buffalo Bill Cody* (Norman: University of Oklahoma Press, 1979), 435.
3. Yost, *Buffalo Bill*, 430.
4. *North Platte Telegraph*, February 23, 1905.
5. *Cody v. Cody* deposition, District County of Sheridan County, Wyoming, February–April 1904, 38–42; Yost, *Buffalo Bill*, 431.

6. Yost, *Buffalo Bill*, 286; Richard Walsh and Milton Salsbury, *The Making of Buffalo Bill* (Indianapolis: Bobbs-Merrill, 1928), 331.

7. Office of Surgeon General, Report, National Archives, RG94.

8. Julia Cody Goodman and Elizabeth Leonard, *Buffalo Bill: King of the Old West* (New York: Library Publishers, 1955), 278.

9. Unidentified clip file, Buffalo Bill Historical Center, Posthumous Memoirs of Colonel William F. Cody, 88.

10. *North Platte Telegraph*, April 14, 1910.

11. Ibid., March 11, 1911.

12. Unidentified clip file, BBHC, Posthumous Memoirs of Colonel William F. Cody, 88.

13. Letter to Julia Cody Goodman from William F. Cody, Buffalo Bill Historical Center, McCraken Research Library, MS6, IIC, Box 1, Folder 5, October 10, 1905.

14. Yost, *Buffalo Bill*, 362.

15. *San Francisco Examiner*, January 11, 1917.

16. Louisa Cody and Courtney Ryley Cooper, *Memories of Buffalo Bill* (New York: D. Appleton, 1919), 323.

17. Russell, *The Lives and Legends of Buffalo Bill Cody*, 469.

18. *New York Times,* January 11, 1917.

19. Yost, *Buffalo Bill*, 399.

20. Cody and Cooper, *Memories of Buffalo Bill*, 324.

21. *North Platte Telegraph*, September 17, 1973.

22. Cody and Cooper, *Memories of Buffalo Bill*, 326.

23. Yost, *Buffalo Bill*, 433.

BIBLIOGRAPHY

Books

Ashton, Dave. *Rosa Bonheur: A Life and a Legend*. Munich, Germany: Studio Publishing, 1981.

Cody, William F. *The Adventures of Buffalo Bill*. New York: Harper & Row Publishers, 1904.

———. *An Autobiography of Buffalo Bill*. New York: Cosmopolitan Book, 1920.

———. *Buffalo Bill's Life Story*. New York: Cosmopolitan Book, 1920.

———. *The Story of the Wild West; Buffalo Bill's Autobiography with Campfire Chats*. Waynesboro, TN: Historical Publication, 1888.

Cody, Louisa, and Courtney Ryley Cooper. *Memories of Buffalo Bill*. New York: D. Appleton, 1919.

Davies, Henry E., and Paul A. Hutton. *Ten Days on the Plains*. Dallas: Southern Methodist University, 1985.

Enss, Chris. *Buffalo Gals: Women of Buffalo Bill's Wild West Show*. Guilford, CT: Globe Pequot Press, 2006.

Foote, Stella. *Letters from Buffalo Bill*. Billings, MT: Foote Publishing, 1954.

Goodman, Julia Cody, and Elizabeth Leonard. *Buffalo Bill: King of the Old West*. New York: Library Publishers, 1955.

Haglund, Kristine. *Buffalo Bill Cody Country*. New York: Bison Book, 1975.

Johannsen, Albert. *The House of Beadle & Adams*. Norman: University of Oklahoma Press, 1950.

Kasson, Joy. *Buffalo Bill's Wild West*. New York: Hill & Wang, 2000.

Logan, Herschel. *Buckskin and Satin*. Harrisburg, PA: Stackpole, 1954.

McMurtry, Larry. *The Colonel and Little Missie*. New York: Simon & Schuster, 2005.

Monaghan, Jay. *The Great Rascal: The Life and Adventures of Ned Buntline.* New York: Bantam Book, 1953.

Muller, Dan. *My Life with Buffalo Bill.* Chicago: Reilly & Lee, 1948.

Musser, Charles. *Edison Motion Pictures, 1890–1900.* Washington, DC: Smithsonian Institution Press, 1997.

Oakley, Annie. *The Story of My Life.* Greenville, OH: Darke County Historical Society, 1926.

Regli, Adolph. *The Real Book about Buffalo Bill.* New York: Garden City Books, 1952.

Russell, Don. *The Lives and Legends of Buffalo Bill Cody.* Norman: University of Oklahoma Press, 1979.

Sayers, Isabelle S. *Annie Oakley and Buffalo Bill's Wild West.* Toronto: General Publishing, 1981.

Walsh, Richard, and Milton Salsbury. *The Making of Buffalo Bill.* Indianapolis: Bobbs-Merrill, 1928.

Wilson, R. L., and Greg Martin. *Buffalo Bill's Wild West: An American Legend.* New York: Chartwell Books, 2005.

Wetmore, Helen Cody. *Last of the Great Scouts.* Chicago: Duluth Press Publishing, 1899.

Yost, Nellie Snyder. *Buffalo Bill: His Family, Friends, Fame, Failures, and Fortunes.* Chicago: Sage Books, 1979.

Periodicals
Billings Gazette Sunday Magazine, February 22, 1976.
Frontier Times Magazine, October 1926, 4–6.
Nebraska State Journal, April 22, 1894.
Real West Magazine, April 1973.

Newspapers
Billings Gazette, December 18, 1979.
Chicago Daily Tribune, February 17, 1905; January 8, 1954.
Chicago Post, June 18, 1893.
The Cody Enterprise, January 20, 1917.

Covington Sun Newspaper, April 16, 1908.

Cripple Creek Times, February 14, 1905.

Denver Post, April 22, 1904; February 28, 1905.

The Evansville (Ind.) Press, June 11, 1927.

New York Herald, February 3, 1901.

New York Press, October 30, 1898.

New York Recorder, "Colonel Cody Talks," May 22, 1894.

New York Times, October 30, 1898; December 25, 1902; June 11, 1909; January 11, 1917; January 14, 1947.

North Platte Independent, February 26, 1903.

North Platte Semi Weekly Tribune, March 20, 1899.

North Platte Telegraph, January 1, 1870; February 23, 1905; June 1, 1905; April 14, 1910; March 11, 1911; June 7, 1952; September 17, 1973; December 18, 1979.

Rocky Mountain News, July 23, 1970.

San Francisco Examiner, January 11, 1917.

INDEX

A

affairs. *See* ladies and infidelities
Alexis, Grand Duke of Russia,
  34–35

B

birth of William, xiii
Bonheur, Rosa, painting of, 85–86
Buffalo Bill Combination, xii, 42.
  See also Buffalo Bill's Wild
  West show; theatrical shows
*Buffalo Bill: The King of
  Bordermen . . .* (Buntline), 33
Buffalo Bill's Wild West show
  Annie Oakley and, 56, 62, 106,
    108–15
  debut of, 52
  encouragement from sisters
    for, 54
  European tours, 62–64, 69,
    77–78, 89
  farewell tour, 121, 123
  financial worries over, 56
  interrupted by death of
    Orra, 54
  North Platte performances,
    51–52, 71
  vision of, 48–49
buffalo hunting
  contests, 27
  expeditions, guiding, 34–35,
    36–37
  of May Cody, 9–10
  of William, xv–xvi
Buntline, Ned, xii, 8, 32–33, 36,
  37–39
burial at Lookout Mountain,
  127–28
Burke, John, 52, 62, 63

C

Carr, General, 29–30
Carson, Kit, xv, 6, 33
Chamberlain Restaurant
  incident, 75–76
Claire, John, 99–101, 104,
  105, 107
Clemmons, Katherine, 75–84
  acting skills, 78
  Annie Oakley, Frank Butler
    and, 78–79, 111
  background, 78
  backing career of, 78, 79–80
  Chamberlain Restaurant
    incident, 75–76
  death of, 84
  divorce proceedings of, 82–83
  end of relationship, 80–81
  Howard Gould and, 81–83
  inciting Louisa's wrath, 73
  Louisa discovering affair with,
    69–70, 76
  meeting William, 70, 77–78
  photograph of, 72
  poisoning allegations of, 83–84
  publicity of affair with, 76,
    81, 83
  testimony on relationship
    with, 96
  William admitting to affair, 93
  William's attraction to, 78–79
Cody, Arta
  birth of, 23
  boarding school and, 66
  death/burial of, 90
  on European tour, 64
  holding grudge against
    William, 89
  long-haired William and, 25–26

Louisa's cruelty to, 64
marriages of, 68, 90
objecting to divorce, 89
photographs of, 17, 38
raising children, 71
relationship with William,
54, 89–90
visiting parents, 69, 70–71
Cody, Charles Whitney, 3–5
Cody, Irma Louise
birth of, 52
boarding school and, 66
catalyst for parents'
reconciliation, 120–21
catalyst for reconciliation,
116–17
death of William and,
124, 128
Louisa's cruelty to, 64,
92, 119
marriages of, 86–87,
119–20
plea for parents'
reconciliation, 98
requesting withdrawal from
divorce, 98
rescuing things from burning
home, 85
visiting parents, 69, 70–71
Cody, Isaac, xiii, xiv, 3, 5
Cody, Kit Carson
birth of, 33
illness and death of, 40–42
letter recounting death of,
41–42
photograph of, 34
Cody, Louisa Frederici
after William's death, 128
argumentative disposition of,
91–92
attending Wild West Show
debut, 52
birth of, 14

blaming William for Arta's
death, 90–91
at Buffalo Bill's shows,
xvi–xvii
consulting psychics, 68
cruelty to children, 64, 92, 119
dealing with infidelities. *See*
ladies and infidelities
death of, 128
dragon's blood (Garfield tea)
incidents, 73–74, 92
dressing William in ornamental
clothes, 34–35
Fort McPherson and, 9, 26,
30–32, 94
hostess skills, 86–87
long-haired William and, 25–26
loyalty to William, xvii
meeting William, 10–16
nephew on unkind behavior of,
66–67
photographs of, 17, 31, 38, 88,
118, 122
poems to, 16
receiving Indian scalp, 47
to Rome, Kansas, 23–24
Rosa Bonheur painting and,
85–86
scolding William for insensitive
behavior, xii–xiii
scrutinizing show ladies,
49–50
at theatrical farewell party,
xii–xiii
threatening to kill William,
73–74
See also divorce proceedings;
marriage (to Louisa)
Cody, Martha, 3, 8
Cody, Mary Ann, xiii–xiv, 5, 8
Cody, Orra Maude, 37, 53,
54, 56
Custer, George, xiii, 22–23, 46, 47

D

death and funeral of William,
124–28
Decker, Mary (May) Cody, 3, 9–10,
44, 48, 90, 121–23, 124, 128
divorce proceedings
Arta objecting to, 89
denial of divorce petition, 98
filing for divorce, 91
infidelities and, 92–93, 96. *See
also* Isbell, Bessie
judge's ruling on, 97–98
Louisa's testimony, 93–95
minimizing publicity of, 91,
95–96
offer for uncontested divorce,
96–97
Orra's death delaying, 54, 56
seeking advice from Julia on,
87–89
trial delays, 91
trial transcript revelations,
91–98
William's re-commitment
after, 98
William's testimony, 93, 95–97
dragon's blood (Garfield tea)
incidents, 73–74, 92

E

early years of William, xiii–xvii
as head of family, 5
learning hunting and
skinning, 2
natural talent with firearms/
horseback riding, 3–5
relationship with sisters, 3.
See also specific sister names
saving sisters from panther, 5
school fight and Mary Hyatt,
1–3
sisters and, 3, 5, 8–10
Edison, Thomas, 62

F

fire, burning house down, 85–86
Fort McPherson, 9, 26, 30–32, 36,
94, 101

G

Golden Rule House, 22
Goodman, Al, 8, 66, 69, 71, 106
Goodman, Julia Cody
on Annie Oakley, 108
caring for siblings, 8
death of husband, 87
jealousies of sisters and, 121–23
Kit's death and, 41–42
letters from William to, 9,
41–42, 43, 46, 51, 87–89,
98, 123
Louisa driving wedge between
William and, 69
marriage to Al Goodman, 8
photograph of, 44
relationship with William, 9, 46,
69, 71
supporting William's career
choice, 43
William/Louisa relationship
and, 10–11, 51, 54, 87–89
William's death and, 124,
126–27, 128
William's long absences
affecting, 66
Gould, Howard, 81–83

H

Helen. *See* Wetmore, Helen Cody
Hickok, Wild Bill, xii, xvi, 22
Hyatt, Mary, 1–3

I

illness and death of William,
123–28
Indians
armed conflicts with, 28–30

bravery in fighting, 29–30
protecting hunting expedition
from, 36–37
scalps of, 6, 26, 46, 47
scouting duties and, 26, 27,
46–47
taken and released by, 27–28
Yellow Hand fight/scalp,
46–47
youngest slayer of, xv
Isbell, Bessie, 93, 100–105,
106, 107

J
judge, William as, 33–34
Julia. *See* Goodman, Julia Cody

L
ladies and infidelities
appetite for beautiful women,
106
Arta holding grudge for, 89
autobiographical account, 50
divorce proceedings and,
92–93, 96
gifts and, 104, 109
Louisa dealing with, x–xi,
xii–xiii, xvii, 42–43, 45,
49–50, 63, 64. *See also specific
names of ladies*
unidentified women at
funeral, 128
William's appealing looks
and, 30
William's testimony/confessions
on, 93
See also Clemmons, Katherine;
Isbell, Bessie; Moses, Mollie;
Oakley, Annie; Piatt, Nadeau;
Sikes, Olive Logan
land deed title spat, 50–51
Last of the Great Scouts
(Wetmore), 71–73, 102

M
Majors, Alec, 6
marriage (to Louisa)
blowup and reconciliation,
47–48
ceremony, 16
common bond of, 68
courtship and engagement,
10–11, 12, 13–16
discord in, 45, 52–54, 56, 63–69
eventful steamer trip after,
17–21
fiscal faithfulness in, 50–51
generosity as issue in, 67–68
growing strong, 32
hardships on children and, 64
house burning down and, 85–86
land deed title spat, 50–51
living in two separate
homes, 67
moving to wild West after, 21
newspaper article on
relationship, 70
restoration of, 117, 120–21
separations during, x–xii,
22–23, 24, 42–43, 47, 66,
68–69
William escaping to plains, 45
William wanting out of, 54
See also Cody, Louisa Frederici;
divorce proceedings; ladies
and infidelities
May, Fred, 75–76
Medal of Honor, xiii, 37
Meyers, Eliza Cody, 3, 5, 9
military service
correspondences during, 16
discharge from, 16
enlisting in, xvi, 8
eventful steamer trip after,
17–21
long absences during, xvi
See also Indians

Moses, Mollie
  blossoming romance, 57–58
  concerns about Louisa,
    57–58
  end of relationship, 60
  joining show, 58–60
  lamenting loss of William, 55
  letters between William and,
    57–58
  maturity of, 57
  meeting, 55–57
  poverty after William, 60
  start of relationship,
    56–57
motion picture, 62

N
New York Recorder article,
  61–62

O
Oakley, Annie, 56, 61, 62, 78,
  104, 106, 108–15
Omohundro, Texas Jack, xii,
  36–37, 43

P
parents of William. *See* Cody,
  Isaac; Cody, Mary Ann
photographs
  of Annie Oakley, 113
  of Arta, 31
  of death documents,
    125, 126, 127
  of Katherine Clemmons, 73
  of Kit, 34
  of Louisa, 17, 31, 38, 88,
    118, 122
  of Orra, 38, 53
  of Scout's Rest Ranch, 110
  of William, viii, xi, 4, 7, 15, 59,
    65, 77, 103
  of William, Arta, and Louisa, 31

of William, Arta, Louisa, and
  Orra, 38
of William, Julia, Helen, and
  May, 44
of William and Louisa,
  38, 118
physical traits of William, ix, 13,
  14–16, 25–26, 35, 61, 75
Piatt, Nadeau, 106
poisoning
  of Katherine Clemmons Gould,
    83–84
  of pet dogs, 92, 94
  of William (by Louisa), 73–74,
    92, 94, 97
Pony Express, x, xv, 6, 7
popularity of William
  first touring troupe and,
    37–38
  gypsy's prediction of, 40
  Louisa resenting, 64–66
  Ned Buntline and, 32–33, 36,
    37–39
  New York Recorder article and,
    61–62
  rise of, 33
  worldwide acclaim, 62–63
  See also Buffalo Bill's Wild West
    Show; theatrical shows

R
*Red Right Hand; or Buffalo
  Bill's First Scalp for Custer*
  (Arlington), 47
Rose, William, 23
Russell, Majors and Waddell,
  xiv–xv, 2–3, 5–6

S
saddles, as gifts, 60, 104
Salsbury, Nate, 52, 87, 108
Scouts of the Prairie (Buntline),
  37–38

Scout's Rest Ranch, 67, 86, 97,
110, 116, 120, 121
Sheridan, General Phil, xvi,
26–27, 34, 36
Sikes, Olive Logan, 105–6
sisters, 3, 5, 8–10, 43, 45, 98,
121–23. *See also* Decker,
Mary (May) Cody; Goodman,
Julia Cody; Wetmore, Helen
Cody
Sitting Bull, 56, 69, 85
Smith, Lillian, 61, 112, 114
stage driving, 11–12
steamer trip, 17–21
Stott, Clarence Armstrong, 87,
119–20

T
Ten Days on the Plains
(Davies), 35
theatrical shows
farewell party, ix–xiii
first, starting new career, 37–38
Louisa scrutinizing ladies of,
49–50
missing family during, 48
reason for beginning, 39
resigning army for, 38–39
sisters supporting career, 43
See also Buffalo Bill's Wild
West Show

train wreck, 106
typhoid fever and dragon's blood,
73–74, 92

V
Victoria, Queen of England, 62–63

W
Welcome Wigwam, 85–86, 116
Wetmore, Helen Cody
death of, 128
at Golden Rule House, 22
hunting expedition and, 9
jealousies of sisters and,
121–23
on Kit, 41
Last of the Great Scouts of,
71–73, 102
photograph of, 44
relationship with William,
6–8
on William and Louisa,
10, 12, 14
on William's character, 54,
71–73
on William's response to house
fire, 85
on young William, 3, 5
womanizing. *See* ladies and
infidelities
women, role of, 61–62

ABOUT THE AUTHOR

Chris Enss is an author and award-winning screenwriter who has written for television, short-subject films, live performances, and the movies. Enss has done everything from stand-up comedy to working as a stuntperson at the Old Tucson Movie Studio. She learned the basics of writing for film and television at the University of Arizona, and she is currently working with producer Howard Kazanjian (*Return of the Jedi*) on the movie version of *The Cowboy and the Senorita*, their biography of western stars Roy Rogers and Dale Evans. Her recent books include *Thunder over the Prairie, The Doctor Wore Petticoats, The Lady Was a Gambler,* and *A Beautiful Mine.*